"[This] book is a valuable and realistic resource on Internet safety that offers a model developed with support from the American Academy of Pediatrics. Parental worries include unwanted sexual solicitation and sexting, exposure to inappropriate information, cyberbullying, and Internet addiction. With its three-pronged approach—Boundaries, Balance, and Communication—this toolkit can be used by parents with children of different ages, from middle school through college."

— *PUBLISHERS WEEKLY*

"As a parent we hear about social media in the news all the time when something bad happens. It can feel like these websites have a whole different set of rules from what we grew up with. We don't often hear about how we as parents can trust the safety rules we know and apply them to these new sites and situations. This is what we need to hear more about. This is what this book delivers."

— Amy, parent of a teen

"So my sister just started high school. I looked at her Facebook last week while I was sitting with her. Her profile pic was her in a bathing suit, and I was like, 'Mary, what are you doing?' I made her change it. Her 15th birthday is next month and I'm getting her this book."

— Sarah, 17-year-old female

"I started my freshman year of college this year, and my parents really want to connect on Facebook. Probably since I'm out of the house and all. I know they don't know much about Facebook or Twitter; they work and have my younger sibs and work and stuff. I told them to get this book so they can figure out some of the basics and make sure my little brother doesn't get into trouble once he is on these sites. He's more of an online gamer now, and I know they sometimes worry about him. This book would help them."

— Todd, 18-year-old male

"I'm a technology coordinator for our school system and help teachers find resources for providing Internet safety to use in their classrooms. I'm always amazed at how different teachers are tasked with teaching this topic—sometimes it's the health teacher, sometimes the computer skills teacher, sometimes the history teacher. What is lacking for us is a comprehensive guide that is evidence-based but flexible enough that teachers can adapt it to use in the classroom. This book works."

— John, school administrator

Ordering

Trade bookstores in the U.S. and Canada please contact
Publishers Group West
1700 Fourth Street, Berkeley CA 94710
Phone: (800) 788-3123   Fax: (800) 351-5073

For bulk orders please contact
Special Sales
Hunter House Inc., PO Box 2914, Alameda CA 94501-0914
Phone: (510) 899-5041   Fax: (510) 865-4295
E-mail: sales@hunterhouse.com

Individuals can order our books by calling **(800) 266-5592**
or from our website at **www.hunterhouse.com**

Sex, Drugs 'n Facebook

>> **A PARENTS' TOOLKIT**

for Promoting Healthy Internet Use

MEGAN A. MORENO, MD, MSEd, MPH

Hunter House PUBLISHERS

Copyright © 2013 by Megan Moreno

Hunter House Inc., Publishers
PO Box 2914
Alameda CA 94501-0914

Library of Congress Cataloging-in-Publication Data
Moreno, Megan Andreas.
Sex, drugs 'n Facebook : a parents' toolkit for promoting healthy Internet use / Megan A. Moreno, MD, MSEd, MPH. — First edition.
pages   cm
Includes bibliographical references and index.
ISBN 978-0-89793-659-0 (trade paper)   ISBN 978-0-89793-660-6 (ebook)
1. Internet and teenagers.   2. Online etiquette.   3. Parenting.   I. Title.
HQ799.2.I5M664 2013
004.67'z80835 — dc23   2012048533

Project Credits

Cover Design: Brian Dittmar Design, Inc.	Special Sales Manager: Judy Hardin
Book Production: John McKercher	Rights Coordinator: Candace Groskreutz
Developmental Editor: Jude Berman	Publisher's Assistant: Bronwyn Emery
Copy Editor: Susan Lyn McCombs	Customer Service Manager:
Indexer: Robert and Cynthia Swanson	Christina Sverdrup
Managing Editor: Alexandra Mummery	Order Fulfillment: Washul Lakdhon
Editorial Intern: Jordan Collins	Administrator: Theresa Nelson
Acquisitions Intern: Sally Castillo	IT Support: Peter Eichelberger
Publicity Coordinator: Martha Scarpati	Publisher: Kiran S. Rana

Printed and bound by Sheridan Books, Ann Arbor, Michigan
Manufactured in the United States of America

9 8 7 6 5 4 3 2 1   First Edition   13 14 15 16 17

≪ Contents ≫

Important Note

The material in this book is intended to provide a review of resources and information related to Internet safety for adolescents. Every effort has been made to provide accurate and dependable information. However, professionals in the field may have differing opinions and change is always taking place. The author, editors, and publishers cannot be held responsible for any error, omission, professional disagreement, outdated material, or adverse outcomes that derive from use of any of the information resources in this book.

≪ Acknowledgments ≫

This book owes much to many. I am first grateful to my patients and their families, who are the inspiration and driving factor for this book's creation. It is really their stories, their concerns, and their insights that led to this book.

I am grateful to my research team who contributed to the book's content, from conducting searches of the relevant scientific literature, to writing and editing content, to helping with the creative aspects of photo shoots and image design. The field of research is heavily reliant on a commitment to mentoring as a way to teach methods and spread knowledge. My research team includes undergraduate students, graduate and medical students, staff, and residents. All are mentees and mentors to each other, and to me. The collaboration I see in our offices every day among the team as well as our growing alumni network is extraordinary and makes work truly enjoyable. My own research mentors have been incredible teachers and role models. In particular, Dr. Dimitri Christakis has always emphasized the importance of taking what we learn in research and then communicating it, not just to the scientific community but also to parents and the patients themselves.

I am particularly grateful to a few key team members who contributed in multiple ways throughout this book—this includes Sara Klunk, Kim Schuchardt, and Megan Pumper. A special thanks is also owed to the team members who contributed their creative eyes and hands to the photographs in this book—this includes Megan Pumper, Shari Schoohs, Sara Klunk, the Schuchardt family, and the Rojecki family, particularly Shannon Rojecki.

I would like to thank the research team for the Adolescent Health in Pediatric Practice (AHiPP) study through the American Academy of Pediatrics. They have been a joy to work with on the creation of the model referred to in this book as the Healthy Internet Use model of balance, boundaries, and communication applied in this book. Led by Dr. Jon Klein, team members who helped develop this model include Alison Bocian, Julie Gorzekowski, Eric Slora, and Donna Harris.

I am grateful to my friends and colleagues at Stylematters, Bob and Suzanne Murray, for transforming this book from an idea into a creation.

I owe so much to my own family: my husband, Peter; our daughters Corinne and Merritt; and the memory of our little Fiona. My parents, Bonnie and Steele, encouraged me to write often while growing up. I still remember taking family trips and having to write a report for each one! My brother Adam and sister-in-law Diane are owed a debt of gratitude for being role model parents and teaching me about patience. My uncle Geoff has been a steadfast source of support and encouragement throughout my own childhood, adolescence, and adult years. I am incredibly grateful to my family for their wisdom, wit, and wackiness.

Introduction

When it comes to the Internet and young people, it's hard to keep up. Yesterday's MySpace is today's Facebook. Chat rooms have been eclipsed by Twitter parties. And while ten years ago young people were *reading* content on the Internet, today they're *creating* it. Figuring out how to keep kids safe online is challenging for many reasons. Technology is constantly evolving and trends come and go. It's often unclear who should be teaching Internet safety to kids. Schools? Community groups? Parents?

In spite of these challenging questions, one thing is clear. Young people need the same kind of guidance regarding Internet safety that they require from adults in all other areas of life, whether the subject is establishing good study habits, determining what it means to have good friends, dating safely, or getting into the right college.

Every day, ordinary kids—our kids—are faced with split-second online decisions. What slang to post on their public Twitter feed? Which spring-break beach photos to upload to Facebook? And whether to disclose yesterday's party hook-up in a casual online comment. Who is going to help these kids make smart decisions? Research done by my research team, as well as others, shows that it's parents who can best and should play a key role in helping their kids to use the Internet wisely. This book will help parents and guardians—and every other interested adult, from physicians to police officers to church leaders—do just that. As we move forward in this book, we will often use the term "parents" to mean both parents and guardians. We hope that other adult role models such as clinicians, educators, and community leaders will find many of the suggestions and information useful as well.

How will we do this? There are three major distinctions about this book to consider before diving in to the chapters that lie ahead.

First, consider the perspectives from which this book is written. As the primary author of this book, I bring the experience and perspective of an adolescent-medicine pediatrician, social-media researcher, and mom. For over five years I've been researching social media, technology use, and online safety among all ages of teens. One of my goals with this book is to bring these research findings to parents in a way that is useful, outside of the academic-journal world where this research usually is published.

But I don't think it is enough for you as a reader to take my word for it. Every research project I've done has incorporated the views and perspectives of adolescents, as research subjects and as student researchers themselves. My research team, the Social Media and Adolescent Health Research Team (SMAHRT) is made up of staff as well as student researchers, and many of our key contributors are themselves adolescents. This approach has helped make our research successful by bringing in key insights from the real experts in the world of social media and technology. For this book, I felt it was important to share perspectives of adolescents who are bumping up against these online safety issues on a daily basis. By incorporating their voices, their experiences, and their expertise, I felt I could present you as the reader with more understanding of what the issues are and what options you have for addressing them. To further commit to our goals of creating a book that could be useful to you as parents, every chapter in this book was reviewed by parents of adolescents. We involved two families in the creation of this book, the Schuchardts and the Rojeckis.

A second distinction is that we have grounded this book in time-less principles of adolescent development. Adolescence is a journey, starting somewhere around age 10 and lasting through about age 25. This journey is made up of different stages, stages that incorporate varied concerns and skills. By attending to these stages, our goal is to ground the information we present to you in issues relevant to your adolescent's stage. In this way, we hope that this book remains useful to you as your teen progresses from a tween all the way to an older adolescent or college student. Further, by grounding the book's content within these stages, we hope that the information can be trusted and leveraged regardless of what new trends in technology may come about.

Finally, we populate this book with up-to-date research translated into practical and usable information. We've included research callouts that discuss specific research studies and what they found, as well as case studies in which one of the book's student-researcher contributors describes an experience that really happened to them. Some of the research was done by my research team, some by others. All of the stories are true and come from adolescent contributors or my patients in my clinic. Thus, when we make suggestions and recommendations you don't have to go on my word for it, you can choose from options guided by what science is telling us about young people, as well as by what adolescents tell us about their experiences, and consider your best options for how to keep them safe online.

The book is divided into three main sections. The first, which includes Chapters 1 through 3, gives an overview of pertinent Internet safety trends and concerns, an understanding of the stages of adolescence as they pertain to Internet use, and an overview of our recommended framework for teaching Internet safety. The second section—Chapters 4 through 10—goes through specific Internet safety concerns including up-to-date research and approaches for parents who may be faced with these issues, or want to prevent them ahead of time. The final section— Chapters 11 through 13—looks to the future to consider approaches parents and adults, individually or in groups, can take to improve the education youth receive about Internet safety. We hope that this three-section framework will provide you with relevant information you can use through your own stages of parenting in the digital age.

The time to help young people learn how to use the Internet safely is now, not later. Studies indicate that to make a difference in teen Internet behavior, we need to provide education *before* the behavior happens. If that window of opportunity is missed, we need to have a plan to provide either new information or reinforcement in later teen years as challenges and opportunities to use the Internet evolve. This book will help you do both, by providing you timeless strategies and a classic framework to support young people of all ages and their safe Internet use.

1

The Wide World of the World Wide Web

Let us be clear from the start. Although the Internet has potential for misuse, abuse, and overuse by young people, the Internet is, well, essential.

Today's youth will need Internet skills for the future. They will need these skills to get jobs, to communicate with others, and to perform many daily tasks. Finding a job today has migrated from being a process of pounding the pavement to a process of searching the web. Communication with old friends used to be done at coffee shops and through phone calls. Now it is accomplished through Facebook chat and texting. Daily tasks such as finding a bus schedule, paying a bill, and planning a trip are all commonly done online. Young people already experience the benefits of the Internet throughout their adolescence. The Web provides a treasure chest of valuable information, available at the click of a mouse. Teens can access far-flung facts and factoids for school papers and find useful explanations of health conditions that can encourage them to take ownership of their own medical conditions or treatment. Parents can get their daily fix from their college-age children through their kids' regular Facebook updates. And isn't it amazing that young people who met at summer camp can now keep in touch easily through e-mail, chat, and social media? Teens in military families who move homes frequently now have new tools to keep in touch with old friends, in some cases with friends all over the world.

Every day, from the classroom to the health clinic to the business world that awaits them, the value of the Internet in young people's lives is evident. But like any form of media—whether pop music, tabloid newspapers, television, or video games—there is room on the Internet for bad things to happen. These may include victimization, overuse, access to dangerous material, and even "addiction." The Internet is a tool, and like any tool the way in which it is used will determine whether the outcome for the user is positive or negative.

We begin this chapter with an understanding that you as an adult are probably pretty aware of the Internet and its many uses. Our goal of this chapter is to provide a brief overview to help lay the groundwork for the information to come in later chapters. We'll begin with answering a few key questions about today's Internet. What are the current trends? What is Web 2.0? What is so social about social media? Or as a parent asked in clinic one day, "How can you tell MyFace from Twit-head?" We will then provide a quick check-in on currently popular sites that young people are using today including Facebook, Twitter, FourSquare, and YouTube as well as gaming and music-sharing sites. We'll end the chapter with some considerations of the benefits and risks of the Internet to help frame what's ahead in coming chapters.

Web 1.0 Versus Web 2.0 »

Just as kids grow to be adolescents, the World Wide Web has grown, too. Its first version was Web 1.0, which has now grown into Web 2.0. What many teens today don't realize about the World Wide Web, though you as parents likely remember this well, is that it wasn't always filled with blogs, Wikipedia pages, and Facebook posts. The Internet began as a place in which information could be accessed. You probably could have found your favorite restaurant's location and menu, or looked at potential colleges for your child and learned a few factoids. Some computer-savvy people even had their own personal web pages with family photos and information about their new dog. The Internet provided a slightly easier way to access and select information that was already available on TV and radio, or in newspapers or phone books. Information flowed in one direction, off the web page and into the viewer's purview; it was a more passive Internet experience. There were not really any opportunities to interact with others, provide feedback, or share.

In 1999 Web 2.0 introduced a new age of the Internet based around the ability to interact with others. Web 2.0 is interactive. It provides the user the ability to work with others and actively have a say in the information provided on the Internet. This new emphasis on interactivity led to a huge culture shift in both the function and culture of the Internet. Information now flows in two directions; it is both viewed and *created* by the consumer.

Web 2.0 has led to what is often referred to as social media, also known as immersive or interactive media. Social media is compelling in that it allows users to become part of the online discussion and information-sharing world. Through a multitude of websites they can communicate in a variety of ways, including through text, photographs, video, comments, and audio.

« Internet Trends

Who uses the Internet? The Internet has transcended cultural, geographical, and socioeconomic boundaries. A report released in July 2011 by the PEW Research Institute found that a whopping 96 percent of teen boys and 95 percent of teen girls use the Internet. Findings among different ethnic groups showed that 95 percent of African Americans, 88 percent of Hispanics, and 97 percent of whites use the Internet regularly (PEW 2011). Internet use is common even among disadvantaged groups, as a study of homeless youth found that 96.5 percent of this group used the Internet (Rice et al. 2010).

As technology and the Internet become ever more integrated into everyday life, youth become exposed to technology at younger and younger ages. I've seen kindergartners skillfully manipulate an iPhone to access their favorite YouTube videos of Elmo. There are applications you can download to your computer or even iPad to entertain your toddler.

With all of the new technological tools that seem to magically appear each year, it can be hard to get a handle on the current Internet trends. Luckily, the Pew Internet and American Life Project has been collecting information on these trends every year since the word "Internet" became a household name. The project is the go-to place for the most up-to-date information on Internet trends for youth. According to the Pew Internet and American Life Project, 77 percent of 12- to 17-year-olds have a cell phone and 74 percent have a desktop or laptop computer (Pew 2011).

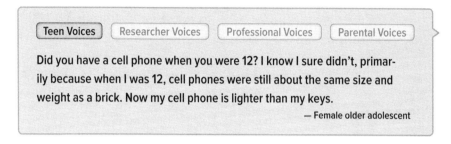

Teen Voices   Researcher Voices   Professional Voices   Parental Voices

Did you have a cell phone when you were 12? I know I sure didn't, primarily because when I was 12, cell phones were still about the same size and weight as a brick. Now my cell phone is lighter than my keys.

— Female older adolescent

The overwhelming presence of technology surrounding our teenagers makes it easier than ever to access the Internet. Over 95 percent of today's teens and young adults are using the Internet, most using it several times a day (Pew 2011). So if most teens access the Internet multiple times a day and can access it through a variety of technological devices, what are they doing online? Perhaps a better question may be what *aren't* they able to do online? Today's teens have been raised in what has been called a "digital society"; they are used to computers and to needing to use them for a variety of tasks. Today's adolescents' use of the Internet can include academic work, communication, entertainment, and socialization. Teens' top online activity is the use of social networking sites, such as Facebook, whereas young adults use the Internet most often to search for information (Pew 2011). This makes sense if you consider that younger teens are very attached to their friends, so their Internet use involves communicating and sharing information with those friends. Young adults and college students, whether they attend a tech school, community college, or four-year university, are

FIGURE 1.1. Cell phones from the vintage days to the present

working and learning, so their Internet use often focuses on information-seeking (Pew 2011).

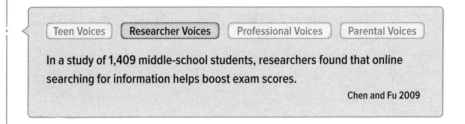

Teen Voices | **Researcher Voices** | Professional Voices | Parental Voices

In a study of 1,409 middle-school students, researchers found that online searching for information helps boost exam scores.

Chen and Fu 2009

Popular Websites Today

As we review popular websites of the current day, keep in mind that these sites may change over time and that different groups of teens may favor particular sites. But an understanding of their similarities and functions can help you as a parent understand their appeal to your teen, and anticipate what future sites may be like.

Some of the most popular websites today are ones that you are likely to be familiar with, such as Google. Google is currently the most used search engine website, meaning it is a website that can be used to find relevant information. Another popular website that most adults are familiar with is Wikipedia, an online encyclopedia whose content is entirely user-generated. Most teens are also very familiar with these websites. We will spend more time here on sites that are more popular among teens, and potentially less known to adults. And we will particularly focus on sites with a social or interactive component brought on by Web 2.0. The interactive features of these sites are often what makes them so attractive and enjoyable, but also can bring some risks depending on who is on the other end of the interaction.

Social networking sites (SNS) allow users to create a profile to represent one's identity, to communicate with other users, and to build an online social network. Let's begin with Facebook, which is undoubtedly something that parents and teens alike hear about on an almost daily basis. At this time, Facebook remains the most popular SNS across all ages, gender, and ethnic groups of teens. With over 900 million users, Facebook is the most widely used social networking site not just in the United States but also around the world. Facebook users establish profile pages where they can represent pieces of their identity in a multimedia format. For example, they can upload photos. Users can also post their Facebook status: A "status update" is a feature that allows users to provide a brief text disclosure, often about what they are doing

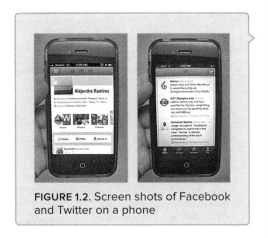

FIGURE 1.2. Screen shots of Facebook and Twitter on a phone

or feeling at the moment. Users can also join—more commonly known as "like"—groups created on the site, such as a sports team, a clothing store, or a company. Twitter, on the other hand, gives its 140 million users 140 characters to "tweet," or post, about anything they want: school, friends, what they had for breakfast, literally anything. Twitter users can also "follow" other users to view and receive updates on their tweets. The Twitter websites describes: "*our goal is* to provide a service that allows you to discover and receive content from sources that interest you as well as to share your content with others." Figure 1.2 shows screenshots from both Facebook and Twitter. We'll describe social media sites in more depth in Chapter 7.

Another popular website today is Pinterest (see Figure 1.3 on the next page). Think of Pinterest as a giant bulletin board made up of a lot of individual boards. On this site users create various "boards" based on different topics or interests such as beauty, cooking, or cute animals. They can also take things they like from other people's boards and re-pin them on their own. Users even have the option of linking Pinterest to their Facebook and/or Twitter accounts, meaning the things they re-pin appear on their profiles for all their other social media friends to see. This feature lets users find which of their friends are using Pinterest as well. Similarly to Twitter, Pinterest lets users "follow" other friends who use the website. And, as with Facebook, those who use Pinterest can "like" other people's pins and comment on them. Pinterest also provides users with a recent activity log, showing which of their friends have either "liked" or "re-pinned" their pins.

FIGURE 1.3. A screen shot of Pinterest

FIGURE 1.4. A screen shot of FourSquare

Next, we have YouTube and FourSquare. YouTube is a website for users to view and upload videos. You can find a video of just about anything on YouTube, from music videos to instructions on how to remove the back cover of your BlackBerry. Some videos are made by companies and uploaded onto the site. For example, you can find old episodes of sitcoms and even full-length movies on this site. Many other videos are user generated, meaning created and uploaded by users. If you go on YouTube and watch videos, you'll notice you don't need to log in or have a password to access the site. YouTube does provide the option to create a profile, but this is only necessary in order to view some videos that contain adult content, or to upload your own videos. YouTube, as a Web 2.0 site, also provides opportunities for interaction. You can rate the videos you have watched and provide comments on them.

FourSquare is a phone application that uses your GPS location to inform you of nearby places, such a restaurants and gyms, based on what you and your friends like (see the screenshot in Figure 1.4). Users can "check-in" when they are at a location, which only involves a click of a button and the GPS does the rest. Checking in allows others to know your current location at that moment, as it posts the information about your current location to the website. FourSquare also allows users to upload photos that are linked to that location and comment on the photos of other users.

Internet Sites with a Social Component

Some websites are not typical social networking sites but have a social and interactive component. Online gaming, for example, used to be an activity that one did alone for entertainment. With many online games today, players can interact and even play against each other. Your teen's opponent can be halfway across the world. Online gaming can range from a simple game of solitaire to an all-out battle against demons to save the universe. There are a seemingly unlimited number of gaming websites, such as addicting games.com, disneychannel.com, and miniclips.com, making it easy for all age groups to participate in the online gaming world. Some online games, like League of Legends (see the screenshot in Figure 1.5 on the next page), Club Penguin, and Diablo 3, even allow users to interact with other players through online chat.

Teen Voices   Researcher Voices   Professional Voices   Parental Voices

A 2010 Neilsen study found that online gambling was more popular than social networking in the United Kingdom.

http://www.bettingcorp.com/online-gambling-trumps-social-media

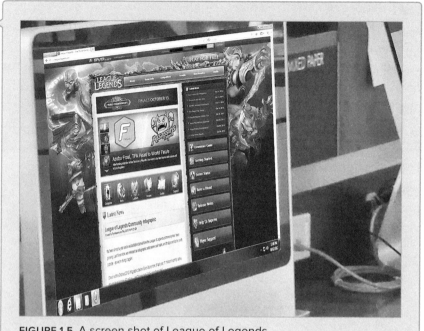

FIGURE 1.5. A screen shot of League of Legends

Music sharing also has a social component. Two popular music-sharing websites at the time of publication of this book are Pandora and Spotify (see the screenshot of Pandora in Figure 1.6). Both require users to create an account, after which millions of free songs are available at their fingertips. Pandora limits the user to a predetermined list of songs based on the artist or genre selected, whereas Spotify allows users to search for and listen to a specific song. If you build a profile of preferences and link to friends, you can receive updates on what your friends have listened to recently. As parents, you may want to be aware that as far as we can tell, there are no limits to what kind of music can be accessed on these sites.

Many of the websites we discussed above are relatively new, and pretty much all of them are younger than your teenager. With people creating new and improved sites every day, what's popular this week may be gone the next. A well-known example of this phenomenon is MySpace. MySpace is a social networking site launched in 2003. It became extremely popular worldwide, which led people to think MySpace was here to stay. That thought quickly diminished, though, as Facebook started to take over as the cool, new SNS on the block. Though MySpace is still around, for many Internet users in 2008, a mere five years later, it was adios to MySpace and hello to Facebook. So, it is important to keep in mind that the examples provided in this book may not always be popular, but the concepts of interaction, sharing, and communicating using the web are likely to remain.

To close this chapter, let's briefly consider specific benefits and risks of Internet use for young people today.

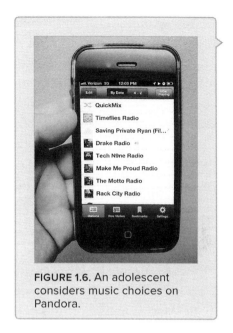

FIGURE 1.6. An adolescent considers music choices on Pandora.

Benefits of the Internet >>

Research, clinical experience, and common sense show us that the benefits of Internet use for young people are wide and varied and include:

- exposure to new ideas and experiences
- access to ready-made platforms to form one's identity in a creative way
- access to knowledge and tools for collaboration
- ease of communication in long-distance relationships
- access to valuable support networks (particularly meaningful for those in racial and sexual minorities)
- participation in community and civic issues and events

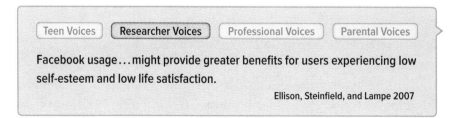

Teen Voices   **Researcher Voices**   Professional Voices   Parental Voices

Facebook usage ... might provide greater benefits for users experiencing low self-esteem and low life satisfaction.

Ellison, Steinfield, and Lampe 2007

Young adults can also use the Internet to get involved with important issues or fundraisers, such as Relay for Life. Relay for Life is a nationwide organization that raises money for cancer research. Those who participate in the 12-hour walk can create a profile on the Relay for Life website. They can then use the Internet to recruit potential donors by sending out e-mails or posting a link to their profile on their Facebook page.

The Internet can be an educational resource and support in the classroom. In one of our research projects, some teachers described the innovative projects they had done in school using the Internet:

Teacher 1: We've been able to use the Internet for classrooms to communicate with another classroom. Kind of the old-fashioned pen-pal-type thing! We've had a lot of success and positive insights that have come back because they [the students] were able to access another group. Right now one group is talking to some school in Massachusetts. Probably never would have met them otherwise but they are doing it online as part of their reading curriculum. It's really pretty cool.

Teacher 2: I've been able to use it to keep a class calendar online so families can keep in better communication with the classroom and also to post weekly newsletters on my website rather than sending them home. Families can go and look at them and look at all the ones in the past, too. And class photos and math games that we play in the classroom, kids can go to my website and play those at home.

Teacher 3: I think because we are in a small town it's great to have the world at the kids' hands; they get a broader view of what's going on. I also think it just makes them better global citizens if they can learn how to especially communicate online with other people. Collaboration, just doing collaboration, and just learning to be better online citizens.

The benefits of the Internet extend to you as parents, too. Parents can use the Internet to keep in contact with their children while they're away at school, camp, or abroad.

The Internet also provides young people new means for organizing and engaging in activism on important issues. In the spring of 2011, local high-

| Teen Voices | Researcher Voices | Professional Voices | Parental Voices |

This past summer, my younger sister went on a two-week trip to Europe with a group of students from her high school. My mother is a natural worrywart, as many parents are, but she was especially nervous about this trip because my sister's cell phone wasn't going to work in Europe. Thanks to the Internet, my sister was able to Facebook message me whenever she could get to a computer. Many big cities have Internet cafés, which made this pretty easy. Then she could let my mom know how her trip was going and that she was okay. She was even able to call us on Skype one night, which I could tell my mom really appreciated.

— Female older adolescent

school students in our city of Madison, Wisconsin, used Facebook to organize a protest walk to the State Capitol in response to Governor Walker's efforts to restrict collective bargaining, which would have a negative impact on these students' teachers. As one of the teen protesters said:

> We wanted to walk to the Capitol to support our teachers, we needed a way to get everyone on board. So we used Facebook to plan the whole thing.

Risks of the Internet »

For every potential benefit of the Internet, a risky flip side also exists. These risks include exposure to information that's incorrect to information that's downright offensive. How many unsuspecting young people have visited whitehouse.com at a peer's suggestion, only to discover porn rather than the website for the President (whitehouse.gov)? Unwanted exposure to sexual content happens; and, then of course, there are young people who spend time on the porn sites by choice.

Other risks of using the Internet include:

- unwanted sexual solicitation
- negative peer influence (e.g., talk on Facebook of getting "wasted" or having casual sex)

FIGURE 1.7. An adolescent checking his Facebook profile

- exposure to online harassment and cyberbullying
- "addiction" (or what the scientific community calls problematic use)
- access to information encouraging violence (e.g., how to build a bomb, buy a gun, commit suicide)

Let's not forget, too, the large electronic footprint that young people leave in their wake. The information they post online is stored and accessible for years to come. This information can be checked by future employers or viewed by friends and peers in one's social media network. Making private information available to the public on the Internet ("Check out my spring break beach photos" or "I slept with so and so last night") certainly creates an element of risk, especially for young people who may not yet have a full understanding of the long-term consequences of their actions.

Ultimately, risks to the young person can come from within, as in the case of Internet "addiction," or from the outside world, as in cyberbullying. People can feel like they are a part of the Internet, wrapped up in the Internet, and even trapped in it (Christakis and Moreno 2009).

What's Ahead in this Book »

Every day, teens and adults alike continue to be wowed and dazzled by the value that the Internet brings to young people's lives. In fact, the ultimate goal of the research done by our team is to make us all smarter about how to help young people minimize risks so that they can enjoy all that the Internet has to offer. This book is designed to help you—as parents and professionals—become smarter, too, regarding Internet safety, so you can successfully support the young people in your lives, day by day.

We conclude this chapter with a few comments from adolescents, young adults, and parents regarding their experiences and advice about the Internet:

> Although the Internet can be overwhelming at times, I have found that it is an invaluable resource for doing well in school, staying in touch with friends and family, and staying current on world events.
> — Female college student

> I think it's interesting how my Internet use has changed as I've grown older. When I first started using the Internet during my early teen years, I remember going on websites like Neopets and Club Penguin. During high school, these websites were replaced by AIM (AOL Instant Messenger) and Facebook. Now that I'm in college, my Internet use is overrun with Google searches and e-mail chains.
> — Male college student

> Throughout my life, as I have grown the Internet has grown with me. The opportunities the Internet has to offer are endless. With that being said, I also have realized the beauty of being disconnected for long periods of time and the effects it may have on wellbeing. Spending extended periods of time without any connection to the world has led me to discover this, and if anyone has the opportunity to do this I advise them to take it. All in all, through my experiences I've come to realize managing your Internet use and finding a balance is key.
> — Female older adolescent

The Internet is my playground. Full of new experiences, friends to contact, and lessons to learn. Every once in a while I may fall down, but the good always outweighs the bad on this virtual jungle gym.

— Female graduate student

It is really astounding to look back just ten years ago and see how many different processes have been simplified by the Internet— searching for information, staying in touch with friends, watching television, and so much more. It kind of seems like as a society we're using the Internet constantly, but there are so many things that used to be difficult, complicated tasks, that we can now complete with a few clicks.

— Male parent

I think it is important as a parent to stay up-to-date with technology as much as you can. Know what sites/games are popular and that your child might be interested in.... Right now it's Facebook, Twitter, Tumblr, Instagram, Pinterest, Minecraft.... My daughter and I went on together to look at these websites and find out what they are about. Several of my daughter's friends who get carried away on Facebook have parents who are not on Facebook and I know do not monitor their child's account. Even if these sites don't interest you personally, learn about them and become interested because they will be in your child's daily life.

— Female parent

 This chapter's contributors included Natalie Goniu.

2

Understanding Internet Use Across Ages and Stages

Teenagers are all basically…well…teenagers, right? As a parent, it can be easy to focus on the more challenging aspects of these young people such as being hard to reach or obsessed with friends. Other times it seems adolescents are superficial, catty, awkward, and confused. Frustrated parents may have additional complaints:

"She locks herself in her room."

"He never talks to me."

"No matter what I say, she won't listen to me."

Sure, these descriptions apply to your kids some of the time, but they do not apply to adolescents all of the time. Teens do communicate quite well in their own ways and on their own terms. Adolescence is now understood as a rich and varied stage of life that begins around puberty at age 12 and lasts through early adulthood at age 25. You may remember being a teen and feeling a sense of relief when you turned 18 and were "all grown up." Why has adolescence suddenly extended into the 20s? Well as it turns out, in the past 10 years scientists have greatly advanced our understanding of the teen brain using magnetic resonance imaging techniques. What we have come to understand is that the brain continues to develop into the early 20s (Casey, Getz et al, 2008). So until the brain is fully developed, your child is still in the stage of adolescence. Brain development progresses throughout adolescence, likely contributing to the many changes that we see during this time period. A 12-year-old does not think in as complex ways as a college student, and we now understand this is related in part to the immense amount of brain growth that takes place during adolescence. Adolescence is truly a transitional period involving changes in the body's growth and development, cognitive skills, social skills, and our understanding of our own identities. It's a huge amount of transition to experience in that 10-year period of time. No wonder teens can get a little moody at times!

In this chapter, we will discuss the finer nuances between adolescent age groups and Internet use. We'll begin by discussing the important early tween years (ages 8–12) when kids are beginning to be influenced by peer groups. We'll then discuss younger, middle, and older adolescents. These changes impact how teens use the Internet, and how you as parents can provide education and guidance that match these stages. This chapter offers insight into how adolescents' growing minds and bodies develop at different points in childhood and the teen years—and then overlays that developmental understanding on Internet use. Let's start by considering differences among adolescent ages and stages.

« Tweens (Ages 8–12)

The tween years mark the time period leading up to adolescence and puberty. During this time, thinking is still "concrete." In other words, tweens take information at face value and believe what is in front of them. Although tweens are able to think about things in a more organized and logical way than when they were young children, they still process information in this literal manner. In clinic I once asked a tween patient, "How did you sleep last night?" and he answered me, "On my back." This is a clear example of concrete thinking.

Kids at this age are very impressionable and likely to believe what they read on the Internet. During this age, children may use the Internet for homework or school activities, but research shows they may be using it increasingly for entertainment as well. This age is also the time when kids show additional interest in their friends and being like them, so these kids may become attracted to pre-teen social networks like Poptropica, Disney's Club Penguin, Webkinz, Sociotown, and Imbee. These websites are geared toward tweens and are more closely moderated than sites like Facebook.

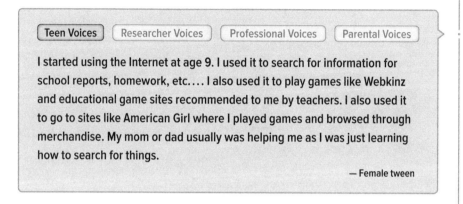

| Teen Voices | Researcher Voices | Professional Voices | Parental Voices |

I started using the Internet at age 9. I used it to search for information for school reports, homework, etc.... I also used it to play games like Webkinz and educational game sites recommended to me by teachers. I also used it to go to sites like American Girl where I played games and browsed through merchandise. My mom or dad usually was helping me as I was just learning how to search for things.

— Female tween

Many parents like you receive questions from their tweens about information they have found on the web. However, unless parents actively seek opportunities to discuss their tween's Internet experiences, opportunities for teaching and discussion can be missed.

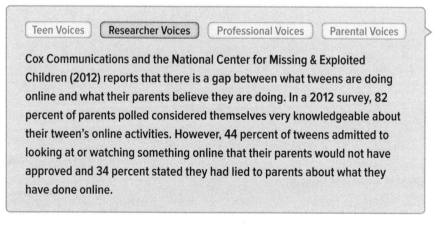

| Teen Voices | Researcher Voices | Professional Voices | Parental Voices |

Cox Communications and the National Center for Missing & Exploited Children (2012) reports that there is a gap between what tweens are doing online and what their parents believe they are doing. In a 2012 survey, 82 percent of parents polled considered themselves very knowledgeable about their tween's online activities. However, 44 percent of tweens admitted to looking at or watching something online that their parents would not have approved and 34 percent stated they had lied to parents about what they have done online.

As this age marks the start of puberty, children may start to use the Internet to gather information about their changing bodies (say, a girl Googling

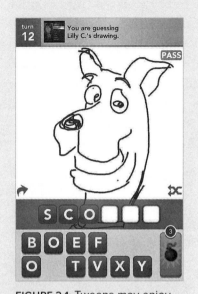

FIGURE 2.1. Tweens may enjoy playing games like "Draw Something" on their smart phones.

"bra" or a boy searching for basic information on masturbation). This is a very normal way to look for this information, as many tweens are embarrassed to ask someone in person about questions related to puberty. However, there can be concerns about whether the information the tween finds on the Internet is accurate and appropriate. One challenge that you may face during this time period is deciding whether or not to provide your tween with a cell phone, especially as many cell phones are smart phones that connect easily to the Internet.

Teen Voices | Researcher Voices | **Professional Voices** | Parental Voices

I so often see this age group playing with their parent's iPhone or iPad when I walk into the clinic. They usually love to tell me about what site they are on and how the site works. Tweens still seem to be okay with their parents having oversight of their online activities.

— Pediatrician Dr. Sarah Rastogi

« Early Adolescence (Ages 12–14)

During middle school, teens may begin to transition from concrete to more abstract thinking. In this stage, adolescents can think ahead and weigh options; they understand how sarcasm and irony work, and they recognize that things are not always what they seem. While these thinking skills are still developing during early adolescence, this developmental stage does not arrive at the exact same time for every adolescent. Puberty is typically in full force during this stage, leading to many questions and potential worries for teens. Body changes during puberty often cause young teens to think about body image and be influenced by what they see among peers or in the media. It's here in this classic, awkward, middle-school stage that young people begin to pull away from their parents; yet even with an increasing peer influence on their lives, kids in this age group are still very open to their parents and other important adult figures' influence. Internet use during this stage often shifts as well. According to the Pew Internet and American Life project data, 92 percent of teens ages 12 to 13 use the Internet (Pew 2011).

> **Teen Voices**   Researcher Voices   Professional Voices   Parental Voices
>
> I am definitely on the Internet more often now—most every day. I also have an iPod Touch and access the Internet through the iPod, not only the computer. I still use the Internet for schoolwork—several of my textbooks are online-only access. I use the Internet for getting ideas for things I want to make, buy, hairstyles etc.... I use Facebook almost daily, and I know that many of my friends use Twitter and Tumblr and Instagram and Pinterest. I don't use these, but I might in the future.
>
> — Female teen

At this stage, if adolescents have not already, they often start to show interest in having their own personal profile on more sophisticated social networking sites like Facebook or Google +. The early adolescent is usually looking for a more individual Internet experience and seems to no longer want to share the family's social site/e-mail.

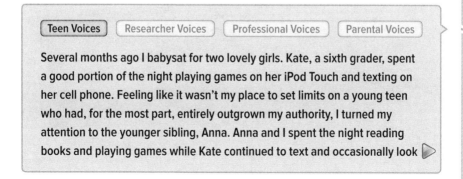

> **Teen Voices**   Researcher Voices   Professional Voices   Parental Voices
>
> Several months ago I babysat for two lovely girls. Kate, a sixth grader, spent a good portion of the night playing games on her iPod Touch and texting on her cell phone. Feeling like it wasn't my place to set limits on a young teen who had, for the most part, entirely outgrown my authority, I turned my attention to the younger sibling, Anna. Anna and I spent the night reading books and playing games while Kate continued to text and occasionally look ▷

over wistfully at Anna and me. Growing up a generation before Kate, I had completed much of my childhood before cell phones and the Internet were introduced into my life. And now, seeing Kate wanting so badly to join us for a game of Uno Attack, I felt sad that her childhood was being cut short by a five-inch screen. After Anna went to bed, I asked Kate if there was anything special she wanted to do. Now lounging in front of the TV, Kate looked up at me and sheepishly asked, "Will you play Uno Attack with me?" We played Uno Attack well past her bedtime, and Kate poured her heart out to me about how everyone in her grade texted on their cell phones and maintained their own Facebook profiles and, because her mom wouldn't let her get a Facebook profile, she felt left out. I tried to assure Kate that her smarts, talents, and kindness defined her far more than a Facebook profile but, ultimately, I sensed that my words were being drowned out by the forces of a digital society. I imagine that many parents struggle with this conflict. How do you preserve your children's youth while being sympathetic to their desires to be accepted among their peers? Do you set limits to try and balance these inputs? Do you set up activities that promote face-to-face interaction? After Kate went to bed that evening, I logged out of my own Facebook, turned off my smart phone, and settled in for the night with a good book.

— Female older adolescent

FIGURE 2.2. With the right guidance, teens of all ages and stages can enjoy a safe, productive Internet experience.

Teen Voices Researcher Voices **Professional Voices** Parental Voices

Teens during this time period are often begging parents for more freedoms when it comes to technology—cell phones, data plans for cell phones, computer access, and availability to be on social networking sites. One of my patients' mothers signed her up for Facebook, but since she was not yet at the age to be able to sign for Facebook they lied about her age. She listed herself as an 18-year-old freshman in high school when she was really a 12-year-old in 7th grade. The patient was surprised about what some of the implications for that might be. Her stepmom brought up to her that people thinking she was 18 and a freshman in high school would also think that she had failed several grades. The patient had not thought of that and decided to wait a little longer to join Facebook until she did not need to lie about her age.

— Pediatrician Dr. Sarah Rastogi

Middle Adolescence (Ages 15–18) »

Once young people move into high school, peer influence takes the lead over parental influence. Most teens can now think abstractly (you parents may notice a good dose of sarcasm from teens this age!). For most teens during this stage, the major changes to their bodies from puberty have taken place, and they begin to turn increased attention toward how to decorate and clothe them. Current data suggests that 97 percent of teens ages 14 to 17 use the Internet (Pew 2011). This age is a key time for experimentation with behavior and identity, and this temptation to "try on new hats" may impact how teens use the Internet. Social networking sites allow teens to create a personal profile, which is an almost perfect platform on which to experiment with one's identity. Uploading pictures and showcasing favorite music allow a teen to construct and revise their virtual identities. A teen this age is all but guaranteed to have one or more social networking accounts and some teenagers may even keep online blogs. Websites like Pinterest, which allow users to "pin" craft ideas, recipes, pictures, fashion ideas, and many other things to their personal "pin boards," are another way that teens express themselves online. Sites like Twitter, which provide rapid information about news, events, celebrities, and other moment-to-moment information bites, also start to gain popularity with this age group (Pew 2011). They often seek out teens like themselves online, teens they may or may not go to school with.

Teen Voices   Researcher Voices   Professional Voices   Parental Voices

It's hard to keep up. Facebook became a "thing" back in 2005, when I was in middle school. When my sister, who was three years older, got Facebook, I remember thinking, "Why would you need that?" In fact, I was perfectly content to chat with my friends, 'soccerboy55' and 'ponygal812,' on AOL Instant Messenger. Then, out of curiosity, I cautiously created a MySpace account under the pseudonym "P from Yugoslavia." Eventually, Facebook extended its audience from college students to the younger teen crowd. I vowed to myself that I would wait until after 9th grade to get a Facebook account. By the time I graduated high school, Facebook had evolved into more than just a social media website—it was a planning tool for every event, a place to learn about anything from local drama to global news and, perhaps most importantly, a prime location for high-school teens to flex their social muscles. In my first two years of college, Twitter exploded on the scene and was accompanied by Google+, Pinterest, LinkedIn, and countless other social networking sites. As a product of the digital generation, I'm the first to admit: It's hard even for adolescents to stay on top of the latest Internet trends.

— Female older adolescent

Teen Voices   Researcher Voices   **Professional Voices**   Parental Voices

One of my favorite things about this age group and their Internet use is the ability for them to find peers with similar interests online. I had one patient who was very interested in anime and was having trouble finding students in his school with the same interest. He went online and found several groups that discussed anime, and he could then share his passion. This patient, who once felt like an outcast, felt like he had finally found a group where he could "fit in."

— Pediatrician Dr. Sarah Rastogi

Older Adolescence (Ages 18–25) »

Adolescents in this age group are young adults. They are more comfortable with how and what they think, with their bodies, and how they look. These young adults tend to select friends and romantic partners based on shared interests and mutual respect, rather than peer influence. Whereas the high school years may have involved shutting parents off from the young person's

---

Teen Voices   Researcher Voices   Professional Voices   Parental Voices

The week before I left for my freshman year of college, the unthinkable happened: My mom friended me on Facebook. My immediate reflex was one of resistance—weren't parents too old to be on Facebook?! However, it turns out it's ok being friends with my mom. She can see what I'm up to and can stay current with the fast pace of my college life. Throughout my freshman year of college, other friend requests from my aunts, uncles, former teachers, coaches, employers, neighbors, and grandparents rolled in. For me, Facebook evolved from a peer-only social circle to a robust collection of all the important people and things in my life.

— Male older adolescent

Teen Voices   Researcher Voices   **Professional Voices**   Parental Voices

College students still use the Internet for social networking but tend to shift their roles from peer networking to networking with groups they might join. They chat with classmates they meet, keep parents and relatives up-to-date with their activities, and also meet and network with future employers. I see college students not only realize the need to protect their online identity but also understand the implications on their future if they don't do so. I have heard several patients mention that they change their name on social networking sites to have more control over their privacy. Patients also describe how they have learned about interesting internships and events through surfing online.

— Pediatrician Dr. Sarah Rastogi

FIGURE 2.3. Older teens often interact and network on sites such as Facebook.

online life, geographic moves away from home inspire some young people in this group to "Friend" their parents and other relatives on Facebook in order to stay in touch. In today's world, older adolescents represent a truly Internet-savvy population; 96 percent of people ages 18 to 29 use the Internet (Pew 2012).

For the remainder of this book, we will use these three ages and stages of adolescence as frameworks for providing information and guidance. Understanding where your child is developmentally and what may be motivating his or her Internet habits can assist you in determining what type of guidance and education to provide at what stages. In the next section, we provide an overview of ways to consider interacting with your child at each stage of adolescence.

≪ Guidance and Discussion Points for Ages and Stages

As parents, you know all too well how the way you interact with your child changes over time. As your toddler showed interest in books, you probably sat together looking at them and the pictures in them. As your child became a preschooler, you may have worked together to find letters in the books and then sounded out words. Your child probably began slowly reading words to you in early grade school, with you providing corrections when needed. Finally, your child was ready to read on his own, with minimal oversight from you. Learning to use the Internet safely and effectively is also an important skill, and your child would benefit from interacting with you as he learns throughout his teenage years. Just as with learning to read, your role will change as your child grows. We will consider the stages of adolescence below with some thoughts on how you as a parent can interact with your child regarding the Internet during that stage.

Tweens >

Because parents still play a starring role in children's lives at this stage, it's an ideal time for you to lay the foundation for good Internet habits, creating a norm that parents are involved in Internet use. This can be done with regular conversations and check-ins, teaching kids how to navigate away from unwanted content, and helping these concrete thinkers recognize that everything found on the Internet may not be true. These guidelines are a good starting point for parents who want to help their tweens have healthy and safe online experiences. Sometimes, however, parents have questions about the Internet that extends beyond these general guidelines. While we don't necessarily have the answers, here are some questions to consider: Should software be installed on the computer to monitor the child's online activity? Should you assume the child knows right from wrong online? These are questions to be discussed as a family. The following thoughts from parents of tweens who posted comments on online parent forums may serve as further points of discussion for your family:

Betsey's approach is to be familiar with the devices her children are using, keep all computers and devices in a common area of the house, and talk to her children about online safety. She writes:

> I don't believe in filtering software. Either it blocks a ton of legitimate sites, or it creates a false sense of security. My kids are 9 and 11, and my approach is simple—all computers in the house are in common spaces, not behind closed doors. Neither of my children have any personal web-enabled devices, and when they use my iPod Touch, they can play games that I've installed (purchased, so no

popup ads) but that's it. They know not to click on ANY popup, even one that claims the computer is broken or infected, and they know that if they stumble across something that's inappropriate, they just close the window. (http://melrose.patch.com/articles/tell-us-how -do-you-monitor-your-kids-internet-use#comments_list)

Lynn feels that software monitoring is a good idea for her tween. Although she has talked to her son about not looking at inappropriate websites, she is worried that he is not listening. She explains:

I have a 12-year-old and an 8-year-old (boys). The 12-year-old has recently started searching for 'naked pictures' online. I checked the history today and it seems he finally got a hit on a very explicit porn site. I want to block his access, not track it. Of course I have had the talk of this is not appropriate, don't do it, etc., etc. (http://forums .ivillage.com/t5/10-12yr-old-Issues-Concerns/Computer-Con trols-Safety/td-p/91098888)

Ultimately, it is up to you as the parent to decide what level of monitoring is appropriate for your child. Tweens with a history of Internet misuse or tweens with special needs, for example, may be good candidates for

FIGURE 2.4. Each parent should decide what level of monitoring is appropriate for his or her child.

software monitoring programs. On the other hand, a tween who likes to communicate with friends and family via the Internet and has established a history of only visiting age-appropriate websites may not need the same level of monitoring. The average family uses five Internet-enabled devices at home, and tweens are increasingly accessing the Internet on mobile devices (Cox Communications 2012). Many parents find it is more effective to discuss online safety as a whole rather than vigilantly monitor each device. Regardless, conversations with tweens should be frequent and honest, and should center on safe Internet practices.

Early Adolescence >

Early adolescence may be the last time that you can play a hands-on role in steering your children's Internet use. It's an essential time to create (or update) guidelines for the young person in this arena. This may involve encouraging young people to balance time online with outside activities, sports, and/or social events, as well as discussing appropriate boundaries around what they will or won't share with others on the Internet. There are 20 million Facebook users under the age of 18 and 7.5 million under age 13 (Consumer Reports Survey 2011). At this stage it is especially important to understand your teen's online persona, who he or she is "friends" with, and how he or she uses the Internet. Many parents feel their child is more Internet savvy than they are. Some parents may even feel helpless. At this stage, there are a lot of unanswered questions. Should you demand to know your child's e-mail and social media passwords? Should you be friends with your young teen on Facebook or request access to his or her account? Let's look at two opposing views by parents of young teens:

Paula's approach is to tightly control her 13-year-old daughter, Shannon's, online use. Although she describes her daughter as a good kid who follows rules and wants to please her family, Paula keeps Shannon's passwords and reads through her e-mails frequently. Shannon had been asking to get on Facebook for over a year and, for a variety of reasons, Paula said no. One day, Paula discovered that her daughter had gone behind her back and opened a Facebook account using just her first and middle name. After confronting Shannon and taking away Internet privileges, Paula began to understand that all of her daughter's friends had Facebook accounts and her tight control was causing Shannon a lot of social distress. After talking to work friends, Paula realized that Facebook was a way to stay in touch, and so she began to think about allowing Shannon to get an account.

Rachel, a mom to a 13-year-old girl, wrote an article in a newspaper describing her desire to have reasonable distance from her child's social life. "Our kids are the first generation of teens to have grown up with instant communication," she says. "Like it or not, they conduct huge chunks of their social lives in cyberspace." For a while, Rachel was online friends with her daughter and her daughter's friends, but she decided that this access was giving her a distorted view of what the girls were really like. She explains, "I've watched most of the children whose pages I was eavesdropping on grow up, and know that they are genuinely lovely, well brought-up and respectful kids who have a good future ahead of them. But I was being exposed to a side of their lives as they try on independence for size that adults really aren't meant to see." In the end, Rachel unfriended her daughter and her daughter's friends. "And do you know what? I've slept an awful lot better ever since," she says (www.dailymail .co.uk/femail/article-2027164 /Facebook-Trust-really-DONT -want-teens-to.html).

FIGURE 2.5. Sometimes younger siblings get exposed to online material earlier by watching their older siblings.

Ultimately, the level of online involvement that you choose to have with your teen is just that— a choice. Although two very opposite points of view are presented here, you can also explore a middle ground. For example, if your teen is worried about you "embarrassing him (or her)" by commenting on his or her online pictures or wall, perhaps an agreement can be made that you will be online friends as long as you keep all interactions offline. Teens this age are beginning the important task of seeking independence. If you attempt to excessively control or monitor their online behavior, they may become resistant, defiant, or even sneaky about Internet use. Instead of reading through all of your teen's e-mails or demanding you have his or her passwords, you could consider asking how your teen's friends and peers are using the Internet or to show you how Facebook works. It is essential to continue to have conversations with children in this age group about online safety and encourage them to ask questions if they are ever unsure about a family rule or a new website. Ideally, teens should feel confident in their ability to stay safe online, but should also understand that they can come to you as parents for help or advice if they find themselves in a dangerous online situation.

Middle Adolescence >

If good Internet habits and communications have previously been set between parents and kids, parents can build on these as their children grow older; if not, parents may have to get creative about influencing their kids' online use. An inquisitive approach can be far more helpful at this stage than a directive one. For example, you can ask questions that prompt your young person to process negative online experiences he or she may have with you as the listener and to ultimately generate solutions that work best for him or her. These are also good years for reminding your teen about the implications of Internet use for his or her personal future. For example, if your teen is considering getting a job or applying to college, this is a good time to remind him or her that teachers, college-admission directors, employers, and other people that he or she wants to impress can easily find Facebook posts, pictures, or tweets online. At this stage, peer influence is a major factor in teen behavior. It is important that you are sensitive to these pressures and allow your teen to navigate on his or her own with an appropriate level of guidance. If a parent uses an authoritarian approach ("Take that picture down right now! What are you thinking? Don't you know employers can see what you post?"), a teen is apt to ignore his or her parent. A different, more-inquisitive approach ("What sorts of things do your friends post online? What sorts of consequences arose from doing that? Do you agree with what they posted?") is much more likely to be well-received. When teens feel empowered to control their own behavior, parents are met with much less resistance.

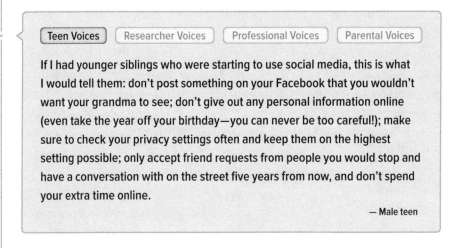

If I had younger siblings who were starting to use social media, this is what I would tell them: don't post something on your Facebook that you wouldn't want your grandma to see; don't give out any personal information online (even take the year off your birthday—you can never be too careful!); make sure to check your privacy settings often and keep them on the highest setting possible; only accept friend requests from people you would stop and have a conversation with on the street five years from now, and don't spend your extra time online.

— Male teen

Older Adolescence

Though you may interact on a less frequent basis than previously with your child when he or she reaches older adolescence, most of these young people start to value Mom and Dad's opinion in a new way—adult to adult. As parents, you can continue to use an inquisitive approach to encourage older adolescents to maintain a balance between online life and offline life and to maintain healthy boundaries when posting online content. At this point, teens are often considered adults by society's standards and are legally in charge of the consequences of their behavior, online and off. If you notice your older adolescent displaying underage drinking pictures or posting inappropriate content on Facebook, you may consider saying something privately to your child and having a two-way conversation about the long-term implications of the behavior. Although some parents may feel they no longer have direct authority over these matters, you should not underestimate how much your adolescent still values your opinion and wants to please you. All parents can feel good about knowing that if Internet safety practices were established earlier, they will have little to worry about at this stage.

A Family Affair >>

Many parents have tweens, teens, and older adolescents in their households. Setting different rules for different age groups is common when it comes to curfews or dating, and it is also acceptable to establish different rules about their Internet use. We asked one tween to discuss the household rules around Internet use to us so we could better understand how different rules may apply to different children in a family.

| Teen Voices | Researcher Voices | Professional Voices | Parental Voices |

Our computer is in the main room of our house. Anybody and everybody walking by can look and know what I am looking at on the computer. I can be on my iPod in my room but only until 9:00 PM. My parents have all of my passwords to Facebook, e-mail, etc.... My homework has to be done before I can use Facebook and my mom is my Facebook "friend." If I change my password or delete my Mom as a friend, I can no longer have a Facebook account. I also had to be 13 to have a Facebook account.

These rules are easy for me to follow—except for the 9:00 PM rule. Lots of my friends are on Facebook after 9:00 and it's the only time we have to message each other.

I have a tween brother and a younger sister. The rules are a little different as they aren't allowed to have a Facebook account. If my little sister needs to find something online, my parents or I usually are helping her. She is allowed to play certain online games, but she doesn't very often. My brother goes online to play Minecraft and look up information for homework.

— Female teen

We asked one family of three teens to summarize the pertinent Internet safety issues by stage. Here is what they said:

Middle School: Believing everything on the Internet, predators

High School: Bullying, photos—not knowing all is permanent, privacy settings

College: New freedom—inappropriate photos and references

FIGURE 2.6. Another benefit of teaching Internet safety when your children are young is that as older adolescents, they can role model positive habits for others.

For many families, teaching Internet safety may be complicated by multiple children in the home at different ages, and with different interests. The strategy that we recommend is starting these discussions at an early age with each child, but allowing the discussions to be adapted to each child's interests and questions. The good news is that once kids are grounded in good safety practices, they are very likely to pass them on to their younger siblings!

Ultimately, you are invested in your child's success. You have your child's best interest in mind and do everything you can to keep him or her safe, happy, and productive. With each generation comes a new challenge for parents. In the 1950s, parents faced the issue of cars and teen dating. Parents worried that their teens would be promiscuous or get into trouble with the law now that the teens had a place for privacy outside the home. Parents had to adjust by setting boundaries, giving a curfew, and knowing who their teen was with during outings.

Today, parents are faced with the additional challenge of Internet safety. Fortunately, helping your child stay safe online is just an extension of what you already do on a daily basis to keep him or her safe in the real world. "Don't talk to strangers at the bus stop" can easily be transferred to "don't talk to strangers online." Just as you already teach your child about having good social skills, being a good citizen, and being kind, you can help him or her apply these skills to the online world. "Don't interrupt someone else when they're talking" can be transferred to "Don't surf the Internet on your phone while other people are talking," or even, "Don't say something online that you wouldn't say in person." Personal presentation—looking your best, creating good first impressions and giving positive lasting impressions—are all skills that transfer from the real world to the virtual world when your child creates that first Facebook profile.

During a research study we did with groups of teachers and school administrators, we heard this insightful quote from a school administrator:

> We were all taught to be safe and self-protective as kids, we were told you don't cross the street without looking or without taking a parent's hand. Maybe one of the earliest lessons is to get permission for what sites you can go to, or how to send an e-mail to Grandma or Grandpa. So maybe one of the first lessons is the limits.

Rather than being overwhelmed by the ever-changing social media trends, ask your adolescent at any stage to help you understand what these sites are and how they work. Your child might be happy to be the "expert" and show you around their sites. It can be a great time to bond with your adolescent and learn about how he or she is expressing him or herself online. By tuning into the developmental issues relevant to a young person, you can meet your young people where they are at each life stage and effectively support them in getting the most out of the Internet.

You do have the know-how to help your children in these settings and, like with other parenting matters, you know when to set limits and when to let out the kite string. Your child will make mistakes online—just like they do in the real world—and as a parent, you will come to understand that they are learning Internet etiquette in the same way they are learning real-world skills. Try to remember that your expectations for your child's online behavior should be aligned with his or her stage of development. The Internet provides wonderful opportunities for academic advancement, social involvement, and fun entertainment. Enjoy exploring the Internet with your teen!

 This chapter's contributors included Mara Stewart and Sarah Rastogi, MD.

3

The Healthy Internet Use Model: Using Boundaries, Communication, and Balance to Stay Safe Online

Almost every parent in the United States knows that someday, as their kids get older, it will be time to talk with them about sex. It can be awkward, it might even be dreaded…but most parents will eventually tackle the "birds and the bees" conversation when their kids are old enough. What happens, though, when it comes to conversations about safe Internet use? In reality, it's just not as much of a tradition to have a safe-Internet talk in the family as it is to have talks about puberty and sex.

When it comes to the safe-Internet talk, some parents have an inkling that the conversation needs to take place. Others make assumptions that it's not necessary. These days it seems that kids have been learning about computers since birth, after all, and they sometimes seem to surpass adults with their ease in navigating the online world. As "digital natives" they should be naturals, right?

Unfortunately, when parents don't get proactively involved in shaping a young person's interactions with the online world, bad things can happen quickly.

Hannah's Story
Hannah was a 13-year-old girl making her way through middle

school like many of her peers. She got *B*'s in most subjects, worked on the school newspaper, and kept busy at night texting with her friends. Then one day Hannah got into a texting match with Caleb. She had recently started flirting with him, after meeting him at a speech competition, and she really, really hoped he liked her back. Then she had an idea. She could send him something to keep his interest going. Hannah took a photo of herself topless with her smart phone and texted it to Caleb.

The end to this story was awkward, uncomfortable, and downright scary; in fact, the situation quickly spiraled out of control. A few days later, a teacher confiscated Hannah's cell phone because she was using it in class, which was against school policy. The teacher found the text with the nude photo of Hannah, and the administration felt compelled to call the police. Since Hannah's new boyfriend lived across the state border (just a few miles away), Hannah, Caleb, their families, and the school were now involved in a case of distribution of child pornography *across state lines*—a felony under federal law.

Hannah's mom never thought her daughter would do something like this; Hannah had always been sweet, respectful, and responsible. Unfortunately, adolescent hormones and her sincere interest in getting Caleb to like her clouded her judgment. After the family was called into the principal's office, Mom felt a bit like a fool. In retrospect, she wished she had had the Internet talk with Hannah *before* this uncomfortable turn of events, not after!

In this chapter, we will discuss the Healthy Internet Use model of balance, boundaries, and communication as part of a three-pronged approach to keeping young people safe online. No parent wants to see his or her child sending or receiving nude photos over the cell phone—or engaging in a variety of other foolish, but possible, online or high-tech activities. Thankfully, by regularly using this model with young people, early on, most parents will never have to!

« Where Are Kids Getting Internet Safety Education?

Internet safety is becoming an increasingly important education topic. However, there is not a general consensus on where it should be taught (in the home or at school?) or who should play a role in teaching it. Should parents hold the highest responsibility? Or can other adult groups, like law enforcement and doctors, also get involved? Our research team conducted a study involving focus groups with those involved in Internet safety education, including teachers, health-care providers, law enforcement, and parents. We wanted to learn more about the barriers these groups face that prevent them from teaching Internet safety, as well as hear their ideas for how to improve the education.

During the discussions about barriers to teaching Internet safety, teachers shared that they didn't feel they had enough training on the subject. One teacher stated:

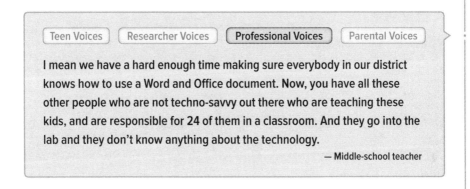

Teen Voices | Researcher Voices | **Professional Voices** | Parental Voices

I mean we have a hard enough time making sure everybody in our district knows how to use a Word and Office document. Now, you have all these other people who are not techno-savvy out there who are teaching these kids, and are responsible for 24 of them in a classroom. And they go into the lab and they don't know anything about the technology.

— Middle-school teacher

Parents and health-care providers also voiced concerns about their personal knowledge on the topic and whether they knew enough about the Internet to teach young people how to use it safely. One thing that all of these groups agreed on was a feeling that there was just not enough time to learn what they needed to know or enough time to be able to have regular discussions with their kids. To make things more difficult, many of these adults shared frustrations that even after they thought they were up-to-date on Internet knowledge, the Internet would change and they'd have to learn a whole new set of information. It became clear to us that there were many challenges for adults in providing online safety guidance and education to young people. An educational framework that was easy to remember, as well as adaptable for changing times and different groups, was clearly needed.

FIGURE 3.1. This teen is so focused on checking Facebook, she forgot to look both ways. The Internet can have a wide variety of risks, some even physical.

« A Model for Keeping Young People Safe

Around the same time that we were wrapping up the research study that illustrated the barriers to teaching Internet safety, a group from the American Academy of Pediatrics approached our research team. This group of researchers, called the Pediatric Research in Office Settings group, was led by Dr. Jon Klein and was starting a research study called Adolescent Health in Pediatric Practice (AHiPP, a "hip" study, right?). They proposed that we work together to create a model that could be used by doctors to guide discussions with their teenage patients about Internet use. The American Academy of Pediatrics is *the* voice for children's health in the United States, so we knew we had a chance to work with some amazing people in the hopes of connecting many new young people and their families with valuable information on Internet safety.

Our goals when developing the model that would be used were clear: We wanted something that parents and professionals could easily recall and reinforce in both scary situations and casual conversations about a child's Internet use. We also wanted to create a model that would be adaptable to all ages of young people and to differing family values. Finally, we wanted the model to be supported by research on Internet use and safe Internet behaviors—not just anecdotes, opinions, or second-guesses.

With these goals in mind, we developed a model that was valid (up-to-date and supported by current research), could stand the test of time, and was easily triggered when an emergency conversation became necessary. After much reflection and many discussions with experts in the field of adolescent health, including experienced physicians and researchers, we chose three essential elements that parents and youth educators could easily incorporate into their Internet safety discussions and efforts: balance, boundaries, and communication.

FIGURE 3.2. Balancing a teen's online and offline lives can be challenging in a technology-filled world, but as a parent you can help your teen do so.

These three elements cover the essentials for encouraging healthy Internet habits: A young person who has the right balance, maintains a good set of online boundaries, and has regular communication with a trusted adult about his or her Internet experiences has all he or she needs to be a safe and happy Internet user. By using balance, boundaries, and communication as conversation topics from the moment a child connects to the Internet, parents and professionals can send an effective and consistent message to young people about how they can interact online in a way that is most beneficial to them. As these topics are reinforced as the child grows, young people will become equipped with the information and skills necessary to be successful Internet users at all stages and experiences of their lives, even when they don't have an adult by their side to offer advice.

< *Balance*

Balance means a healthy equilibrium exists between a young person's online and offline activities. Consider these examples, which point to various issues involving *imbalance*:

- a college student who stays up till 4:00 AM most weeknights playing the new game he just downloaded to his iPad and then begins to miss morning classes in order to sleep in late

- the high schooler who is unable to leave her cell phone in her school locker because she feels a need to check her texts during class time

- the tween who accepts everything he sees online as reality rather than considering it could be a representation of one viewpoint or even a false statement

Each of these scenarios points to the issue of imbalance. Let's look a little closer now at healthy balance and begin to define what it really looks like.

We consider a healthy balance as spending enough time to constructively participate in today's online world without tipping into the realm of concerns, such as reliance on the Internet as a sole source of socialization, as feelings of withdrawal when away from the Internet, and as "excessive" time spent on the Internet. The American Academy of Pediatrics' guidelines for children is to avoid spending more than two hours a day using online media; however, it remains unclear how these recommendations translate to teens and young adults. In our model, we have intentionally decided *not* to quantify healthy balance using exact time limits for this older age group. We think it's more appropriate for young people (tweens and up) to discuss with you as their parents what degree of balance works best for that particular young person at that stage of development. For example, while one young person may be able to handle two hours of high-tech or media time across the day, another might do better with far less. It depends on the young person—his or her personality, "constitution," maturity, health status, and situation.

There are several ways to consider balance in your own setting. Does the tween's personality become altered after too much time playing video games? Can the college-aged student retain an upbeat attitude if she's been in her dorm room for a long time playing around on Twitter? Do the parent and high schooler feel comfortable with an online marathon of video watching over winter break but agree that this doesn't work well on a normal school week? In our view, the answer depends on the situation, family goals and values, and the young person.

Even without an exact defined threshold for when balance tips over into imbalance, imbalance between online and offline worlds can and most definitely does occur. Adults often start to sense that imbalance when they see or hear their teens talk excessively about their involvement with online activities. Young people often describe a "gut feeling" they get when their Internet use becomes more than they intended. Parents, pay attention to these feelings or instincts, and trust them. They often mean it's time to have a conversation with your child and to enforce some balance between online and offline worlds. In such situations—or ideally before—parents can help young people consider that there are simply times that it's important to turn the Internet off and be fully present in the "real world." Some easy times that can be enforced as "offline time" include during meals, during classes at school, or at bedtime. You as parents and adults may also take time to educate young people about what can happen if they do tip the online–offline balance, for example, by neglecting a homework assignment or falling asleep in class because they stayed up too late playing an online video game. Failing grades or a bad high-school transcript (leading to fewer college acceptances) are also real possibilities that parents can help the young person think about. At its worst, imbalance can start to head in the direction of Internet addiction (or what researchers call *problematic Internet use*).

Finally, when we talk about balance, note that we aren't just talking about the amount of time spent online—we are also referring to developing a young person's ability to understand that what they see and feel *online* might impact what they see and feel *offline*. Without the critical thinking skills that are needed to balance the things they see online, young people may consider the risky, hurtful, or even dangerous things they see online as *okay*. Does the young girl who frequently visits the blog about ways to lose weight start feeling worse about her body? After watching a YouTube video of an older boy attempting the Cinnamon Challenge, where he tries to swallow 1 tablespoon of cinnamon with no water, does the group of young boys having a sleepover partake in this dangerous challenge? These are both examples of ways in which the ability to balance and differentiate what you see online with how you act and feel in the offline world is certainly needed.

It may not seem like it much of the time, but most young people will take to heart the advice you offer about balancing their Internet time. We often hear from college students we know or work with—digital natives who were in middle school or high school when Facebook was created— that they wish they had received more guidance from parents or at school on the best ways to use the Internet.

Boundaries

A young person who knows how to balance time online with time offline is on his or her way to using the Internet in a healthy way. But even with the perfect balance, a young person may still find him or herself being pressured by an online friend to do something uncomfortable or questioning whether to accept a Facebook friend request from someone unfamiliar. These are just a couple of examples where the issue of boundaries may come into play.

Many things could go on the list of online situations where a young person would benefit from boundaries:

- When the young person is online, what is he doing with other people and how well does he know those people?
- What photos does she post publicly and what information does she make public that should be kept private?
- Does he share his passwords with friends or acquaintances?
- What type of information does she seek using the Internet, and are some topics considered out-of-bounds in her family?

These are all questions that relate to boundaries, the second element of the Healthy Internet Use model.

Just like adults, young people have the right to make conscious choices about how they interact online—to draw boundaries around things like what videos they will watch, what information they decide to share, with whom they share this information, and how they respond to the information they come across. Most of us would agree that young people need to learn to set boundaries in the offline world; we think it's equally as important that they learn to set boundaries in the online world.

Emily's Story

Emily was a pudgy, happy-go-lucky twelve-year-old who was mildly cognitively disabled. She often acted developmentally younger than her age; as a result, Emily's mom thought she had a few years before she needed to teach her daughter about appropriate online boundaries. Emily seemed too young to get into any real trouble on the Internet. Then one day Emily came to her mom and said she wanted to meet an online friend in person. He was an adult man. Emily's mom quickly realized that the boundaries conversation had to happen right away!

Although Emily may not have understood the dangers of meeting this new online friend, she asked her mom for help in meeting him. Even in those elusive and rebellious teenage years, young people look to parents and adults they trust for guidance.

It's probably obvious to you that boundaries are very important for young people. The hard part might be figuring out what these boundaries should look like online and how you can work with a young person to help him or her establish and maintain them. Let's start with some examples of what online choices young people might face at different ages of their lives.

For tweens, early in their Internet interactions, they might face the choice of what websites to visit, which social networks to join, and what kinds of information they should be allowed to enter when signing up for a new online account. These types of choices are best met with good knowledge about which types of information are okay to share and which are not.

For a middle or high school student bombarded by peer pressure, the choice might involve whether to join friends in the online harassment of a fellow student, whether to post certain photos of oneself or friends online, and what kinds of information are okay to share in social media posts. During these same years, parents with a teenager at home may talk about relevant boundaries for keeping information about upcoming vacations off of social networking sites to avoid potential burglaries. A guidance counselor might talk with a young person about his or her online choices and how they can impact future job or college opportunities, while a physician during a well-child visit might offer advice about what kind of information is best to keep private on social media.

We also can't forget about college students, who are often living outside the close supervision of their parents for the very first time. In this new situation, sometimes exciting and oftentimes uncertain, this group is also trying to fit in with their peers. They might be faced with the choice of posting images of themselves online doing activities that they think will help them fit in better—like smoking at a hookah bar or playing a drinking game. When faced with each of these different choices, these young people would benefit by having a set of boundaries that they can use to help navigate these tricky choices, now that they are away from home.

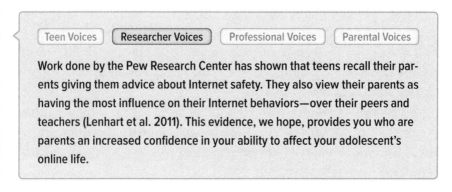

Teen Voices   **Researcher Voices**   Professional Voices   Parental Voices

Work done by the Pew Research Center has shown that teens recall their parents giving them advice about Internet safety. They also view their parents as having the most influence on their Internet behaviors—over their peers and teachers (Lenhart et al. 2011). This evidence, we hope, provides you who are parents an increased confidence in your ability to affect your adolescent's online life.

Given these research findings, we also hope you will ultimately feel empowered to establish clear and practical boundaries with your child early on and to ensure that certain "no-cross" zones are put into place *before* problems happen. When children are young, we tell them not to speak with people they don't know or with people who make them feel uncomfortable. As our children get older, we teach them how to be respectful of all people and how to navigate situations where there is pressure to do something they don't want to do. You probably have taught your child important lessons about how to present oneself in social settings and what types of behaviors are considered rude or mean. When approaching discussions about online choices the core issues remain the same, it is just the environment where the child might face these choices that has shifted. Putting these boundaries into place at an early age—as you would do with other safety behaviors, such as explaining to a child that it's unsafe to run into a busy street—is essential to keeping kids safe. It also sets the standard that you'll be involved in supporting your young person online as he or she grows and develops, which should make things easier down the line.

Communication >

The idea that balance and boundaries keep kids safe online is important. But these tools only work if ongoing communication is also present between young people and adults. Good communication is often the best means for encouraging and maintaining both balance and boundaries. This is where communication—the third and final element of the Healthy Internet Use model—comes into play. Like so many issues in life, it all comes down to being able to talk to each other: parent to child, teacher to student, doctor to patient, psychologist to teen client. The best way that you can support young people in staying safe and healthy online is by keeping the channels of communication open.

We included communication as one of the three elements of the Healthy Internet Use model because of the impact that parent–child communication has on many other types of adolescent behavior. For example, the frequency (number of times) of conversations about alcohol that parents have with their adolescents has been shown to impact alcohol use in college (Patock-Peckham et al. 2006; Walls et al. 2009; Windle et al. 2008). In short, the more parents talk to their children about being careful about alcohol use, the less those kids are going to abuse alcohol in college. Two-way communication with a young person about establishing appropriate Internet habits is likely just as important as the communication you have with a teen about his or her alcohol use.

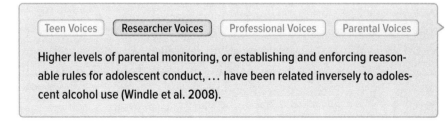

Teen Voices · **Researcher Voices** · Professional Voices · Parental Voices

Higher levels of parental monitoring, or establishing and enforcing reasonable rules for adolescent conduct, ... have been related inversely to adolescent alcohol use (Windle et al. 2008).

In addition to talking about safe Internet use with kids and teens, creating a comfortable environment for communication at home, at school, and in the community makes it easy—or easier—for young people to discuss online problems or challenges they encounter; They may see something on their Facebook page (e.g., a mean comment from an acquaintance) or become upset about a poor grade they received on a test after spending a good amount of time the night before chatting with a friend online instead of studying.

Typically, we envision that communication as taking place in person, but occasionally we've discovered that technology can actually facilitate this kind of communication as well!

Travis's Story
Travis was a 16-year-old who had been getting into yelling matches with his dad ever since he had been caught drinking vodka at a friend's house. In the middle of one of these fights, Travis walked out of the kitchen and escaped into his room, then closed the door. Suddenly, his dad's phone dinged with a text. It was Travis, saying, "I'm sorry. I really am. I just need u to lighten up a little." His dad paused for a minute. He found himself agreeing with Travis, too, that he could stand to give him a little more space. He texted back, "I'm sorry too. It's just that I've been worried about you."

And so the conversation continued far more productively than it had in person. Sure, it took place via text, but it was real communication, and it worked as a crutch while Treyvon and his father rebuilt their trust in each other—that day and for the next few weeks as well. Over time, Treyvon and his father's communication about how they felt and what they were worried about migrated from text messages back to in person conversations.

Because kids are beginning to use the Internet at younger and younger ages, you may want to put communication patterns in place early on, so that they can continue as the young person grows. Parents may sit next to their four-year-old as she plays on a Disney website for the first time and discuss baseline rules with her, such as explaining that she can play until the timer in the kitchen goes off and talking about what games are okay for her to play.

In situations like these, parents can start a dialogue with simple questions, such as what the child likes about the website. Teachers can talk with their young students about the school rules for using on-site computers and what rules they have at home. Health-care providers have a unique opportunity to talk with parents and their young patients about the time their patients are spending online, what websites they might like to visit, and what they should do if they see something that makes them feel uncomfortable.

As young people move through adolescence, you can shift from a more directive approach to a more inquisitive one that respects young people's autonomy and encourages them to find solutions for themselves. For example, parents might ask their teenager if he has seen a classmate being bullied online and whether he thinks it is okay to bully someone over the Internet. These conversations may be held at the dinner table, where younger siblings can listen and begin to consider these issues as well.

Other adults can play a starring role in promoting balance, boundaries, and communication. A guidance counselor might talk with a high-school

FIGURE 3.3. Setting rules about when it is and isn't OK to use technology may be worth consideration. Dinner time, a time that fosters interaction among the family, may be a good place to start limiting phone use.

student about how she thinks her time spent online might be impacting her grades, or about how a student's Facebook profile may impact her college applications. A physician might help a teenage patient establish a plan to make sure he is getting enough sleep at night, which might include putting the phone or computer someplace far away from the bedside.

There are many ways that you can offer relevant and useful advice that will point young people toward healthy online behavior. As young people get older, your focus can shift from simply giving advice to opening up dialogue. In the chapters that follow, we will offer possible conversation starters that you can use when talking to a young person at home, at school, in the clinic, or during a safety presentation that will help them reflect on their current online choices and point them toward better choices, if necessary.

« New Directions for Internet Safety Education

To provide young people with safe and productive online experiences, parents can't be solely responsible for teaching Internet safety. This chapter has described a model for teaching healthy Internet use that can be used by parents, as well as adapted and used by teachers, health-care providers, and community leaders. It is our hope and intention that the three concepts in the model can be adapted into different lessons and learning activities.

From our research, we learned that although many different groups voiced different opinions about certain aspects of Internet safety, the groups all agreed that Internet safety was a shared responsibility and not just the responsibility of a school or of parents. Here are a couple of our favorite quotes.

> The thing is, hitting [this topic] from various fronts. You know not just hitting it from school. Hitting it at the doctor's office and hitting it at school and having the parents at least included somehow.
> — Female law enforcement official

> Who has a stake in all of this? Well gosh, society does. So where does it fall? I guess I keep going back to schools because that's where society does the educational component, that's a big part in that. Now

can the police help with that? Sure. Can the medical profession help with that? Sure. And they can do different things.

— Male parent

Thus, we hope that the Healthy Internet Use model will be of use in your home, as well as in your community. It is worth knowing that national organizations, such as the Federal Trade Commission and Common Sense Media, have offered educational resources including presentation templates and school curriculums. These organizations offer lessons and educational materials that can be used and adapted by parents, teachers, and other adults invested in teaching Internet safety education.

P.S.—It's Ok to Enjoy these Conversations »

Conversations about safe Internet use don't have to be awful or awkward. Really! Instead, they can become integrated into natural, everyday conversations that you have with your child (or young person) during those little

FIGURE 3.4. Conversations about Internet safety don't have to be serious and glum. This father and daughter share a laugh as the father explains that "face books" *used* to be paperback books handed out in school with all the students' photos in them.

moments that come up throughout the week: when your tween waits with you to create a login (setting up a user name and password) for her favorite site, when your teenager tells you during the drive home from soccer practice about a friend who's meeting an online acquaintance in person, or when your twenty-something complains over winter break that she'd rather be on Facebook than going to Grandma's house for dinner. Each of these moments are opportunities to learn about the young person's interests and wishes, build trust, ask questions, and offer guidance. As an adult, you may feel like a digital novice, but you certainly shouldn't shy away from these discussions because you feel like you don't know enough about what kids are doing online to offer good advice. These young people are looking to you to help them steer through these online experiences, and you have plenty of expertise to address problems that may arise. By keeping balance, boundaries, and communication in mind, you can help young people get the most out of the Internet without it ever "getting" them.

 This chapter's contributors included Kaitlin Bare, Suzanne Murray, and Libby Brockman.

4

You Saw *What* on YouTube?
Handling Exposure to Unwanted Material Online

From Google to Yahoo to Bing, youth today have a vast expanse of fascinating and informative material at their fingertips. Gone are the days of slogging through heavy, glossy-paged encyclopedias to write up a report on monarch butterflies or eighteenth-century architecture. A few flicks of the computer keys and a swift click on a mouse, and young people have at their disposal hundreds of pages of content related to their search string. Or is it really related? And, if it is related, is it useful, appropriate, or accurate?

In this chapter we address exposure to two major areas of unwanted online material. The first is exposure to material that is *inappropriate*. This type of material may include information that is not appropriate for your child's age, such as finding sexual content when your tween is trying to look up where to buy a jock strap for baseball. Inappropriate material also includes information that you would not want your child exposed to at *any* age, such as pornography, violence, or drugs. As teenagers continue to use the Internet for various activities in their daily lives, it is likely that, at some point, they will come across something that is unpleasant or makes them—or you!—feel uncomfortable.

The second type of unwanted material that your child may be exposed to online is material that is *inaccurate*, or false. An example of this type of situation may be if your college-age child is looking up information about how much cold medicine to take, and finds information on medication doses that are incorrect or out of date.

« Exposure to Inappropriate Information

There are areas on the Internet that are just not appropriate for children or teens. Not surprisingly, these sites often include sex, drugs, or violence. Sexual websites include those in which viewers can see or read sexual content, such as images featuring nudity or text describing sexual behaviors. Other sites provide opportunities for interaction. On this type of site your child may be requested to engage in sexual activities or sexual talk, or to give personal sexual information. Information about substance use may be featured in many formats. Descriptions of experiences while on drugs may be published on blogs, videos about how to roll a joint may be found on YouTube, and photographs of peers drinking beer may be posted on Facebook. Teens may also come across violent material showing grisly footage or promoting aggressive behavior. Exposure to these sites may be unintentional, or intentional.

< *Unintentional*

When thinking about unintentional exposure to inappropriate information, parents often wonder: *How can exposure to this type of content happen? Aren't teens the digital-native generation?* However, particularly among younger teens, these situations can come up quite often. Young teens going through puberty often have many questions about the changes in their bodies and feel embarrassed asking their parents or their health teacher. That young teen may decide to do a Google search of a topic such as, "Is masturbation normal?" or, "Do I need a bra?" What will he or she find? A list of websites may just pop up on the screen that display videos of masturbation, or lingerie advertisements. What started as a legitimate inquiry into a developmental issue can, in a nanosecond, yield information that can be alarming or disturbing to the younger teen. And this unwanted exposure to inappropriate material can even occur when the teenager is researching a completely unrelated topic. Some common typos (such as mistyping a web address) or other simple mistakes (such as accidentally downloading pictures while downloading games) can lead to a teenager viewing unwanted material.

FIGURE 4.1. "We don't say that word in our house!" Younger siblings may get inadvertent exposure to inappropriate words or risky content while observing older siblings.

Intentional >

Although many teenagers who view inappropriate material do so unintentionally, the Internet also provides an avenue for teens to actively search for and learn about dangerous activities. Violent websites can easily be

FIGURE 4.2. The Internet allows teens to access information about anything imaginable, even material that is inappropriate.

accessed, from YouTube videos depicting gang violence to websites showing how to make a bomb. According to one news story, a 14-year-old boy faced felony charges after setting off homemade bombs in California. He learned to make the bomb, which was made from common household supplies, by watching a video on YouTube. Fortunately no one was hurt, but the blasts were reported to be powerful enough to seriously injure someone (KTLA News 2010).

Sometimes, even teens who choose not to engage in risky behaviors may use the Internet to better understand the activities of their peers or what they have seen in the media. As teenagers transition into young adults or move away from home, they are often curious about the behaviors they foresee themselves encountering in the near future. It isn't only search engines that function as resources for these teens. Interactive media such as videos on YouTube or social comparison with friends' Facebook profiles can lead to exposure to inappropriate material.

Teen Voices | Researcher Voices | **Professional Voices** | Parental Voices

During college I worked as an orientation leader for incoming new students to a large University. I never ceased to be surprised at the wide range of questions these students would ask, from the best places to eat on campus and the most interesting courses to enroll in, to which bars allow the most underage patrons in and places where marijuana can be purchased. While students often do not wish to engage in these behaviors themselves, they are interested in understanding the lay of the land in their new surroundings. Frequently, these students express that the only exposure they have had to what "college drinking" looks like is through media: television, movies, and online. Several students who had avoided alcohol in high school expressed an interest in initiating substance use once they arrived at college. Even with the intention of drinking in a safe and responsible manner, albeit underage and illegally, the only content that these students have accessed typically depicts extreme scenarios with mostly, if not entirely, positive outcomes of alcohol consumption.

— Male graduate student

Exposure to Inaccurate Information »

The world of Web 2.0 means that every Internet user has the potential to be both a viewer of information, as well as a contributor of information. The Internet has allowed anyone to be a writer, anyone to voice an opinion, anyone to share his or her voice. The sheer volume of information is staggering! Online information contains a mix of facts and opinions, truths and falsehoods. How is a teen, or an adult for that matter, supposed to figure it all out?

Consider this:

A Google search for "flu" led to 148,000,000 results.

A Bing search for "diet" led to 513,000,000 results.

A Yahoo search for "puberty" led to 42,900,000 results.

Information that is posted on the Internet often does not include references or citations to establish its initial source. More than a few online sites can include a mix of facts and interpretation of those facts, or include opinions or beliefs about those facts. These mixed websites can be very

FIGURE 4.3. Even older adolescents can be overwhelmed by the vast amount of information on the Internet.

confusing to interpret. Further, websites may not have been updated recently, so the information on them may be old or out of date.

[Teen Voices] **(Researcher Voices)** [Professional Voices] [Parental Voices]

Though parents and guardians may rely on the Internet for information, many users may overlook useful information because of the web page's lack of appeal. In 2012 SMAHRT (Social Media and Adolescent Health Research Team) completed a study that evaluated the quality of 70 websites found in an online search for Internet safety terms. We looked at factors such as whether the website listed the authors of the information and how recently the website information had been updated. We looked at how cluttered the website was and whether there were advertisements present. Among those websites, the average quality score was 5.5 on a scale of 0–14. Based on these results, we suggest that Internet users take a moment to access if what they are reading is actually accurate and reliable information.

When looking for information online, be sure to assess quality factors of a website as well. Hints that a website provides dependable, quality information may include:

- lists of sources or citations to back up the facts
- the authors' names as well as their credentials
- the date the website was last modified
- few, if any, sales or advertisements
- links to reliable sources

If sources or references are listed, be sure to check them out—this can be a good way to double check that the information you are reading is trustworthy and accurate.

In some cases, misinformation may lead to a lower grade on a social studies test. In others, it can be dangerous or nearly deadly. One *USA Today* story tells of Lucky O'Donnell, a 19-year-old who used the Internet to research cocaine. He looked at different websites to determine how much he could take and in what combinations with other drugs without getting sick. O'Donnell ended up in the intensive care unit after combining cocaine with Tylenol PM and alcohol. Later, he reported that "one site said it was fine, one site said it wasn't. I wasn't able to differentiate the information. You want to believe everything you read" (Leinwand 2007). This example clearly combines the problem of finding both inappropriate and inaccurate information!

Frequency of Unwanted Online Exposure »

Nearly all teens use the Internet for a variety of reasons each day, and most will likely run into some type of information at some point that is either inappropriate or inaccurate. Previous research tells us:

- One in 3 youths report unintentionally being exposed to sexual material online, and 1 in 7 report receiving unwanted sexual solicitations (Wolak, Mitchell, and Finkelhor 2006).
- Thirty-eight percent of youths reported exposure to violence online (Ybarra, Mitchell, and Korchmaros 2011).
- Fifty-four percent of social-networking-site profiles of 18-year-olds included references to sexual content, substance use, or violence (Moreno et al. 2009).

Although anyone who uses the Internet is at risk for coming across unwanted material, there are some characteristics of teenagers that make them more likely to view this material. One research study found that more boys than girls encountered unwanted sexual material. Youth over 15 years of age and youth whose family's income exceeded $50,000 also had more exposure to unwanted material (Mitchell, Finkelhor, and Wolak 2003). The same study also found that the more teenagers use the Internet, the more likely they are to be exposed to unwanted sexual material. The same is true for teenagers who use the Internet at other households or have access to e-mail. The researchers involved in this study concluded that this increased activity by teens all suggested more extensive and exploratory use of the Internet. Those who use the Internet to search for health information (Rideout, Foehr, and Roberts 2010) or use file-sharing software to download images also are more likely to come across this material (Wolak, Mitchell, and Finkelhor 2007).

‹‹ The Negative Consequences

Content on the Internet is particularly influential for teenagers and college students, especially if it is posted by their peers. This is often called user-generated content, and it is often interpreted by teens as being accurate or true. Videos on YouTube, for example, that are made with a shaky hand or capture candid timing create a perceived authenticity that encourages teens to interpret the video as truth. Professionally produced content, such as movies, often show risky behaviors. In comparison to videos of friends or other teenagers who are capturing their "daily lives," the peer-produced video likely holds much more weight in the mind of a teen.

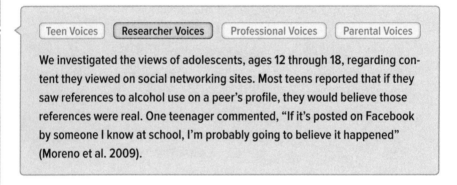

Teen Voices   **Researcher Voices**   Professional Voices   Parental Voices

We investigated the views of adolescents, ages 12 through 18, regarding content they viewed on social networking sites. Most teens reported that if they saw references to alcohol use on a peer's profile, they would believe those references were real. One teenager commented, "If it's posted on Facebook by someone I know at school, I'm probably going to believe it happened" (Moreno et al. 2009).

There are a couple theories that suggest why this content is influential to teens. While we don't do a lot of theorizing in this book, these two are worth knowing about as they can help you to understand the power of these Internet displays and the reasons that they may be compelling to your teen. These theories have often been applied to adolescents' exposure to attitudes or behaviors on media, such as television, movies or music, and can also be applied to the Internet. The Internet, which can include television shows, movies (blockbuster movies as well as user-generated ones), and music, also includes text, images, and video created by peers.

One of these theories, called Bandura's Social Learning Theory (Bandura 1994), has been around for decades. This theory describes how teens may learn about and try behaviors after seeing someone else do that behavior, either in real life or in the media or on the Internet. One example would be the teenager who watches a friend skateboard down a huge hill without falling. Whether the teen saw this behavior down the block in your neighborhood, or on YouTube, seeing this behavior modeled successfully by someone else increases the likelihood that the teen will try it.

> [Teen Voices] [**Researcher Voices**] [Professional Voices] [Parental Voices]
>
> We recently investigated content of alcohol-related videos on YouTube related to college. Some examples of behavior-modeling videos included large social groups of teens drinking at many times of the day. Videos included phrases such as, "all is fair in love and blackouts," and "there is a time and place for everything, and it's called college." The videos mostly showed positive consequences of drinking, such as social popularity and sexual encounters. Even the videos with negative consequences used humor to counter these outcomes.

A second theory, called the Cultivation Theory (Gerbner et al. 1994), explains that certain behaviors in the media can be more powerful to teenagers when the behaviors exceed what the teen has been exposed to in life. For example, sex. Most younger teens have limited exposure to sexual behavior in real life, so exposure to this behavior in the media can be very powerful and lead to changes in attitudes, intentions, or even behaviors. The theory argues that exposure to content in media or on the Internet can shape the teens' attitudes and expectations to be more consistent with what they see in the media or on the Internet than with what they see in real life.

The concepts described in both these theories are supported by research. Research studies have shown that teenagers who had repeated exposure to online pornography had more permissive sexual attitudes (Braun-Courville and Rojas 2009; Moreno et al. 2009). Further, youth who indicate that many of the websites they visited showed real people engaging in violent behavior were significantly more likely to report behaving violently (Ybarra, Mitchell, and Korchmaros 2011).

These theories, research studies, and examples show the important role that you can play in discussing and interpreting the content that your kids encounter on the Internet. Fortunately, there are many tools that parents can use to stay informed and provide guidance to their teens as they navigate the muddy waters of the Internet.

« What Parents Can Do

The Healthy Internet Use model can be applied to exposure to unwanted material, both in cases of inappropriate and inaccurate information.

‹ *Balance*

To teach your child how to handle the likelihood of encountering inaccurate information on the Internet, parents can remind teens to seek information from various sources. Teens can weigh the information they see online with what they learn from other sources, such as teachers, parents, and print media. This skill can also apply to viewing information that peers display on social media. Parents can remind teens to balance what they see peers saying on social media with what they know about their friends from offline experiences.

‹ *Boundaries*

As parents, you can set expectations of Internet use, and check that those expectations are working and still apply.

You can begin by discussing the content of this chapter with your teen, and explaining what inappropriate and inaccurate websites are and how one may be exposed to them.

FIGURE 4.4. Parents can talk to their tweens and teens about what sites they are viewing and set guidelines for how the site should be used responsibly.

You can provide a set of rules for the types of material that are off-limits. Some parents find it useful to use the analogy of how R-rated movies are off-limits at certain ages.

You can also provide a set of steps that a teen can follow if he or she stumbles onto an inappropriate site, such as immediately closing that window, and letting a parent know about the situation. Here is some advice from a teen to younger tweens:

> I'd tell them not to click on random things that they come across— they don't want to get a computer virus or see something weird. Also I would tell them not to type in random words on Google Images because it's too easy to see stuff you shouldn't see. Stick with playing games and researching for schoolwork with Mom or Dad.

Communication >

When children are younger, you as parents can begin discussing how the Internet is a large public space; it can be filled with content that is not always appropriate or meant to be viewed by everyone. Young people should be taught to trust their gut. If they come across something they think might not be appropriate for them, it probably isn't, and they can make the choice to leave the page.

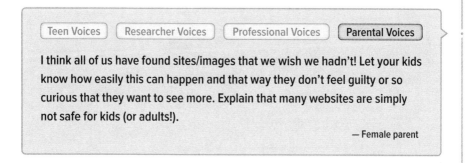

> | Teen Voices | Researcher Voices | Professional Voices | **Parental Voices** |
>
> I think all of us have found sites/images that we wish we hadn't! Let your kids know how easily this can happen and that way they don't feel guilty or so curious that they want to see more. Explain that many websites are simply not safe for kids (or adults!).
>
> — Female parent

At the same time, you as parents can promote an environment where your child feels comfortable talking to you about how he or she feels after encountering unwanted or frightening material online. Communication channels need to be open, and check-ins can happen often. These check-ins can be part of checking in on other parts of your child's life, including situations like these:

"How did your report on the Oregon Trail go, Jeff? Did you have any trouble finding content on the web? What type of information did you find? Did you think any of it was inaccurate? How could you tell?"

"You mentioned that Sasha's mom let her get a Facebook profile, but she got in trouble for posting inappropriate pictures. What did you think when you saw those pictures? Why do you think that content is inappropriate?"

 **Parents' Toolkit**

Here are some conversation starters to use with your teen:

- What do you think might happen if you search for something that isn't an appropriate topic for teens your age to be searching?
- What steps can you take if you find something online that you don't think is appropriate?
- Have you ever searched for something in Google or YouTube and found something that you weren't looking for? What did you do when that happened?
- Has anything you've seen online ever scared you or made you feel weird? What do you think you could do differently so you don't get that feeling again?
- What types of things have you seen online that surprised you or made you wonder if they really happened?

Here is an exercise to try with your child:

- Google a search term, such as "college drinking" while sitting at the computer with your child. This is a great exercise to do with your teen as they are near the end of high school or in college.
- Notice how the Google search engine starts to "auto fill" what it anticipates your term will be. How could that auto fill lead to incorrect searches?
- Look at the variety of information in the top search terms. Some links are to health information about preventing dangerous drinking. Another site is a study that looks like it is presenting college drinking as a positive behavior. Discuss how a single search term can lead to such a variety of information. How can you pick the sites to click from such a varied list?

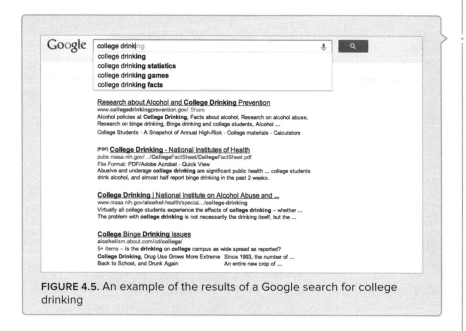

FIGURE 4.5. An example of the results of a Google search for college drinking

- Pick a site and look at it together (see the example in Figure 4.5 above). Does the site include the authors, or the credentials of the site creator? What are signs of a credible website?

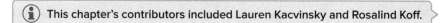

ⓘ This chapter's contributors included Lauren Kacvinsky and Rosalind Koff.

5

Sex on the Web

Sex on the web—whoa, a loaded topic to be sure. There are two facets to this topic that we will cover in this chapter. The first is sexual predators and the second is sexting, both of which are areas of concern for parents. Though you as a parent surely hope your child will have neither of these negative encounters, many young people accidentally stumble upon disturbing Internet content, while others intentionally seek out websites that are inappropriate for kids—and even for adults. At the same time, some reputable organizations have worked hard to provide safe and accurate sexual health information online for teens who can't find out about this topic any other way. Online sources with accurate sexual health information is the third topic that we address in this chapter. Clearly, this is a hot topic and one that is difficult to discuss; we'll do our best so that you can too.

Online Sexual Predators

Any one case of sexual predation is one too many. Unfortunately, online sexual predation happens fairly often, as 13 percent of children have been solicited sexually by older adults or other youth. One in 25 youth have been solicited aggressively, including attempts to make contact offline. And similarly, 1 in 25 youth have been asked to take provocative sexual pictures of themselves. Two of 3 teens were frightened or upset by these encounters, and many responded by ignoring or blocking the attempts or leaving the websites following an attempt.

It can be difficult to think of the Internet as a space that has the potential to create a predator–prey dynamic, but without caution and care, teens can fall into the trap of a sexual predator. A sexual predator is a person that attempts to initiate sexual contact with another person through a coercive and manipulative manner, and an online sexual predator uses the Internet to initiate these relations. Who are these predators? Research has shown that online sexual predators are more likely to be Caucasian males that are unemployed and single (Babchishin, Hanson, and Hermann 2011). Many predators target a particular group—either by age, race, or gender.

There are typically thought to be four types of online sexual predators, although as the characteristics of the Internet and predators change, these definitions may change as well. The first type is called a collector; this is usually an entry-level offender who collects images of children through the Internet and Internet pornography. Second, we have travelers, also known as voyagers, who are predators that engage in online chat with children and subsequently "groom" their victims by gaining trust. Travelers eventually try to coerce children into meeting up with them. Next, there are the manufacturers—individuals who produce child porn and frequently have criminal histories as sex offenders. The last type are called chatters. Chatters target victims in chat rooms and build a trusting relationship. They use this trusting relationship to elicit sexual talk and behaviors via the use of web cameras. Clearly, online sexual predators pose a threat to young and vulnerable Internet users.

Many parents have the idea of an online sexual predator as someone who is dishonest and violent in luring teens into sexual behaviors, but this is often not the case. Predators often present themselves as friendly and socially enticing adults. One study found that only 5 percent of online sexual predators pretended to be teens themselves when inviting teens to participate in sexual behaviors (Wolak, Finkelhor, and Mitchell 2004). Sexual predators often take the time to invest in a process called "grooming," which engages teens and allows them to feel as if a meaningful relationship has been developed. Many victims develop an emotional attachment to the predator, and in fact, 73 percent of face-to-face sexual encounters are followed by another sexual encounter (Mitchell, Finkelhor, and Wolak 2005). As tweens, teens, and young adults form their sexual identities and romantic relationships as a normal part of growing up, it is important to ensure that this process is occurring in a healthy manner.

Teen Voices | **Researcher Voices** | Professional Voices | Parental Voices

Crimes Against Children Research Center at the University of New Hampshire reported that in 2009 the arrests of sex offenders who used the Internet to meet victims decreased. However, arrests increased for sex offenders who used technology to facilitate sex crimes against minor victims who they already knew face-to-face (Wolak, Finkelhor, and Mitchell 2011).

Inconsistent Internet Monitoring

In March 2012 Facebook scanning software identified conversations about sex between a 30-something man and a 13-year-old girl. Facebook employees immediately contacted the authorities and the man was charged with soliciting a minor. This type of scanning, however, does not guarantee safety. Failures in incident monitoring have led to sexual solicitation on Facebook and MySpace, as well as Skout, a smartphone app designed for flirtation with nearby strangers, and Habbo, a teen-oriented virtual world gaining popularity (Mann 2012).

There are certain factors about a teen that may alert an online sexual predator to vulnerability. Teens who have been found to be most vulnerable to online predators tend to be new to Internet etiquette and online activity and uneducated as to the dangers they may face. They also tend to be more trusting, attention-seeking, isolated, or lonely. Another group that may be at-risk includes those who try new things such as risky behaviors, or those that are confused as to their sexual identities.

Chatroulette

Sometimes called "extreme social networking," Chatroulette is a chatroom website that began in 2009. It involves randomly matched short sessions of video chatting with strangers across the globe (see Figure 5.1 for a screenshot from a YouTube clip that shows the general layout of the site). Celebrities occasionally hop on to surprise

FIGURE 5.1. This screen shot is from a YouTube video released in September 2012 on a spoof of an extremely popular song, called "Call Me Maybe" by Carly Rae Jepsen. The dual screens show what the chatroom website Chatroulette looks like for users; one screen shows your actions and the other shows the random person on the other end of the video chat.

fans, enticing more and more tween and teen users to join. However, this site has also been called a "predator's paradise." Though the site asks that individual's confirm they will not engage in predation, these guards can easily be bypassed, and it is difficult to prosecute predators who may have logged on from another country. While the site required individuals to be at least 16 years old to join, parents may want to consider restricting the use of Chatroulette and similar websites until at least age 18 (Miller 2012).

What Parents Can Do to Prevent Sexual Predators »

There are many ways to interact with your child regarding his or her Internet use and to prevent negative consequences. The Healthy Internet Use model provides three important concepts to keep in mind as you navigate conversations with your child.

< *Balance*

It's normal for kids to want to meet new people and make new friends on and offline. However, as they grow older they must balance the excitement of their increased freedom with the challenge of choosing their social circle with safety. You can reference tried-and-true safety messages such as, "don't talk to strangers," and how those rules apply to the online world.

< *Boundaries*

As your child begins to explore social networking sites, be sure to set guidelines on how your child should be socializing online. For example, kids should never download images or files from an unknown source. You can go through the steps of creating social networking site profiles with your child and explain the importance of creating screen names and e-mail addresses that do not reveal gender or personal information. You can then walk your child through the process of setting security limits on their Facebook, MySpace, or Twitter accounts. Some families set rules that no one in the family should ever have an online friend that is not known offline. Other families set rules that anytime their child wants to meet a new online friend face-to-face it needs to be at home when parents are around.

< *Communication*

Again, the most important thing a parent can do to help keep their child safe from Internet sexual predators is maintain open lines of communication. Tell your child that they should come to you if they ever encounter something online that makes them uncomfortable. Remember that while

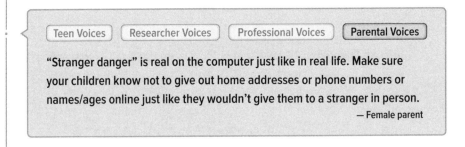

Teen Voices   Researcher Voices   Professional Voices   **Parental Voices**

"Stranger danger" is real on the computer just like in real life. Make sure your children know not to give out home addresses or phone numbers or names/ages online just like they wouldn't give them to a stranger in person.
— Female parent

some teens are naïve about the dangers of the Internet, others are not and simply need help making the connection that these dangers could happen to them.

Sexting »

The term "sexting" refers to sending, receiving, or forwarding sexually explicit messages or pictures, typically over a cell phone or the Internet. This may include sending a nude, or semi-nude picture through e-mail, or posting a provocative message through Facebook. Most teens who engage in sexting do so either to try to gain attention or interest from a potential romantic partner, or in the context of an existing romantic relationship. Many teens who send a sext mistakenly believe that the only person who will view that sext is the person who receives the message.

FIGURE 5.2. An example of a "sext"

It's surprisingly challenging to figure out how often this behavior occurs, both because of teens' reluctance to disclose the behavior due to embarrassment or fear of getting in trouble, and because of different definitions of what a "sext" really is. One patient in my clinic told me she "hadn't really sexted" because she sent nude pictures of herself through e-mail, not via text, so it "didn't count." Research has given us some insights into the frequency of the behavior; one study found that 20 percent of teens have sent or posted nude/semi-nude photos or videos of themselves. A 2012 study found that 28 percent of teens had sent a sext, and 31 percent had asked someone else for a sext (Temple 2012).

Who is at risk for sexting? New research suggests sexting can be considered within the framework of adolescent sexual behavior. In the 2012 study by Temple, researchers found that adolescents who engaged in sexting behaviors were more likely to report they had begun dating and engaged in sexual activity compared to those who did not sext (Temple 2012). For girls, sexting was also associated with risky sexual behaviors. So does this mean that if you catch your daughter sexting that she is also having sex? Definitely not. But it does mean that if you find out your teen has been sexting, and you haven't already had "the sex talk," it is time to do so right away.

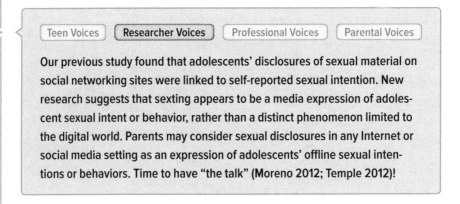

Teen Voices   **Researcher Voices**   Professional Voices   Parental Voices

Our previous study found that adolescents' disclosures of sexual material on social networking sites were linked to self-reported sexual intention. New research suggests that sexting appears to be a media expression of adolescent sexual intent or behavior, rather than a distinct phenomenon limited to the digital world. Parents may consider sexual disclosures in any Internet or social media setting as an expression of adolescents' offline sexual intentions or behaviors. Time to have "the talk" (Moreno 2012; Temple 2012)!

« How Parents Can Prevent or Deal with Sexting

Setting boundaries and communicating are the key components of the Healthy Internet Use Model to help prevent and deal with sexting. Talk with your child about setting clear boundaries about what is acceptable and what is not, and why your family has such rules. Centering such messages on respect or self-esteem can be a helpful way to frame your messages so that your teen knows *why* this is such a big deal.

Mariella's Story
Mariella is a 17-year-old whose phone was confiscated in English class. Her teacher found semi-naked photos of Mariella on it and called her parents. When discussing this difficult situation with Mariella that night, her mom told her how much she loved and respected her. She explained that she hated to think of someone else

seeing those photos and having that person lose respect for her as a result of seeing these photos. Mariella's dad explained how these photos might be interpreted by a potential partner, or friend, or even by an uncle or friend's parent. Mariella's protests and defenses quickly turned to tears and embarrassment, and the three of them began a difficult discussion about the rules they would use in the future.

Communication: As Mariella's story illustrates, setting boundaries and having good communication on this delicate topic are both challenging but doable. Many teens engage in sexting because, quite frankly, they probably have never been told that they should not do so. Most parents are reluctant to talk with their kids about sex, and sexting may be an even more awkward conversation as many parents are not sure what it is! Parents can approach this conversation with confidence in their understanding of safety and family values, and feel ok about being inquisitive about their teen's views and experiences about sexting. An example conversation is:

Mom: "I want to talk to you about something and I'm pretty sure this is going to be an awkward conversation. So I'd like about 20 minutes of time to talk in the living room and then you can go back to what you're doing."

Jordan: "Awww Mom."

Mom: "No, really. What I want to talk to you about is sexting. I'd first like to know if you've ever heard of this."

Jordan: "Uh, yeah. I heard about it at school."

Mom: "Well, I'd like you to tell me what you think it is."

Jordan: "It's when you send a nudy picture over a phone, right?"

Mom: "Yes, it can include any type of sexual picture or text sent by text, e-mail, or on the Internet. What do you think about this?"

Jordan: "I don't know. I'm not sure why people would do that."

Mom: "I'm glad to hear you say that. Some people think that you could get someone to like you that way. But there are a lot of problems that can be caused by doing this. What do you think those might be?"

The conversation may end with a reinforcement of the rules of the family about that topic. A follow-up conversation a couple days later, just to check if there are any questions, can also be helpful.

≪ Sexual Health Information

On the brighter side of sex on the web, there is a great deal of helpful, useful, and appropriate information out there that can help your child make responsible and safe decisions. If you think back to your years as a teenager, you probably remember wondering about sex. A lot. You may have wondered when was the right time to have sex, or how to protect yourself from pregnancy, or how to learn the risks of sex. As much as we want to keep our children from growing up too fast, the reality is that "my little girl" or "our boy" will likely begin to wonder about sex during the teenage years. More than 4 out of 10 high school students report having had sex, and about a third of high school students are currently sexually active. Yet among those students, only 60 percent are using condoms to protect themselves when they have sex (CDC 2011).

As a parent, your biggest concern is your child's safety. That's why you're reading this book! So if your child is wondering about sex, planning to have sex, or having sex, they need to be safe in order to prevent pregnancy and transmission of sexually transmitted infections (STIs). And whether teens are having sex or not, they are curious about it. And with today's technology, whenever teens are curious about something, they are likely to turn to the Internet for help. Questions may include:

- "Is my penis/vagina/breasts/body normal?"
- "I think I might be gay. What do I do?"
- "How do I know when I'm ready to have sex?"
- "What if I don't want to have sex with my boyfriend but he does?"
- "What is sex like? How do I do it 'right'?"
- "How do I put on a condom?"
- "I think I might be pregnant…"

Teens may have had sex education of varying degrees in school, but when they want answers to their deepest, darkest questions and don't want

FIGURE 5.3. The Internet provides a way for teens to receive answers to their questions while remaining anonymous, or at least feeling like they are anonymous.

Teen Voices | **Researcher Voices** | Professional Voices | Parental Voices

In 2010 we investigated how teens search for sexual health information online, and the challenges they face. Some of the quotes from participants showed that they had trouble figuring out how to find useful information:

"It's hard to look up questions like that without coming across porn."

"You have to type [your search] in right. Like if you just type in "the pill," it's not gonna show a birth control pill, it's gonna show a whole bunch of pills. You just have to type the right thing."

In addition, we found that it's difficult for teens to find resources for sexual health information that are written at their level of understanding. Teens explained:

"I mean, okay, we're not illiterate either, we can read, but.... I'm not going to understand [a long scientific] word. And that could be a major point... that [word] could be the whole cure thingie right there and the answer to your question" (Selkie 2011).

to ask an adult, they may turn to their friends. And very likely they will also turn to the Internet. Using the Internet is a simple, anonymous way for teens to ask questions that they would otherwise be too uncomfortable to ask their parents, friends, or doctor. By far their search efforts can be summed up in one word: GOOGLE.

Using Google (or another search engine) to find sexual health information has advantages and disadvantages. On one hand, search engines can be used to find answers to specific questions and are an easy way to access a large number of resources for big questions. The problem comes when teens are trying to sort through this large amount of information. Chapter 4 discusses the challenges of accessing online information that is both appropriate and accurate.

How Parents Can Approach Sexual Health Information on the Web

Since it is common for teens to look online for answers to questions that seem embarrassing, parents can provide guidance to their children in how to interpret the information that is found. Applying the three approaches of the Healthy Internet Use model can help you as parents guide your children's Internet use.

Balance
As a parent, you can encourage teens to balance information gained online with that learned from other sources, such as health class. You can also encourage your teens to bring the information they find online to their doctor during their next visit, as many physicians are used to, and comfortable with, assessing and interpreting information that patients find.

Boundaries
You can reinforce boundaries on what type of sites are ok to use for sexual health information; this may include medical sites such as WebMD or sites for a specific hospital or clinic. Remind your child how to recognize sites that are unlikely to include appropriate or accurate information.

Communication
While this may be hard to do, talk with your child about sex. Sex is one of the toughest topics that a parent can address, and including the Internet

side of sexual behavior can make the subject a bit more challenging to discuss. But research shows that the efforts are worth it, as kids whose parents have talked with them about sex are less likely to initiate sex at an early age and less likely to engage in risky sexual behaviors. The effort, the embarrassment, the uncomfortable situation—it's all so worth it.

A Parents' Toolkit for Sexual Conversations

A few years ago, SMAHRT researcher and medical student Meaghan Trainor worked with a group of teachers to create the BILDS model of communication. BILDS stands for Brainstorm, Investigate, Listen, Direct, Self-esteem. When starting a conversation with your child about sex on the Internet, it can be helpful to use the BILDS conversation model to "bild" lines of communication. Consider the following questions to prepare for and guide your conversation.

B—Brainstorm >

What do you want to know from your child? Why may they go to Internet sites that are risky? Who are they talking to online? What does your child already know about your expectations about the Internet and about Internet safety in general?

I—Investigate >

If you are going to have a conversation about a topic as charged as sexual content on the Internet, you probably want to do research to learn more about what teens are doing on the Internet. Reading this book is a good start, but get online yourself next. If you don't know the language of Twitter—read up on it. It's important to educate yourself so that you can give your best answer to any of your child's questions that pop up.

L—Listen >

Nothing you tell your children will register if they do not get enough time to tell you their side of the story or what they know. If you don't understand something they are talking about, ask them to tell you more about it. Frame your questions in a humorous way when appropriate, i.e., "When I was your age we were still using paper cups and string to talk with our friends. Can you tell me what you mean when you say you were 'creeping' last night online?"

D—Direct

If you aren't direct with your child, your child won't be direct with you. Tell your child exactly what you observed or what you are afraid of; otherwise you may never get the meat of your message across. By "direct" we do not mean bossy or commanding. The most important thing you can do for your child is help him or her come to the right conclusions on his or her own. Being direct will help keep confusion to a minimum.

S—Self-Esteem

Use any and all conversations with your child as an opportunity to talk about self-esteem and self-image. Many times when kids are acting out online they are looking for positive affirmations of who they are. This does not mean you should provide praise at all costs. Provide precise praise and help them think about who they are and who they want to be, and whether they are portraying themselves online as that person they want to be.

You Can Do This!

It's important for you as a parent to help your teen navigate the wealth of sexual health information available on the Internet. Maintaining open communication about this information is key, as with all aspects of Internet use discussed in this book.

A good starting point is to think back to your own teenage years and think of the questions about sex you had at the time. Then go ahead and search for that on the Internet! This way you can see what your teen is probably finding with their searches as well. If your teen asks you a question about sex, ask what your teen knows about it already and how he or she got that information. Offer to help look up information on the Internet. See the "Resources" section at the end of the book for some excellent resources for you and your teen.

FIGURE 5.4. The Planned Parenthood website is an accurate and informative resource for answers to sexual health questions.

To end this chapter, we leave you with a story from a male adolescent:

During high school I had my first girlfriend and things were getting serious. My sister told me that my mom was worried that I was thinking about having sex. Well, I was. My mom was acting all weird around me and I was dreading the talk I figured we would have. I thought my mom would tell me to break up with my girlfriend. One morning my mom was making breakfast and I went by the computer and saw that the Planned Parenthood page on condom use was on the screen. I was so embarrassed, all I could do was yell, "MOM! SERIOUSLY?!" and go to my room until she left for work. When I got home from school that day she was still at work and the site was still up on the computer. I looked through it and, well, I learned a couple things that they didn't tell us in health class. I left the site on a different page so my mom would know I had looked at it. At dinner that night she smiled at me, and it seemed like we both knew it was ok. It was ok.

ⓘ This chapter's contributors included Dr. Ellen Selkie, Meaghan Trainor, and Megan Pumper.

6

Cyberbullying and the Invisible Black Eye

In the old days, kids passed notes in class—elaborately folded rectangles of lined paper with long-hand scrawls confessing love, telling secrets, or creating gossip. Today, kids send "notes" via text, instant messaging (IM), Twitter, and Facebook. Using these new technologies, information is still shared, judgment is sometimes passed, and relationships are forged and broken. Just as interactions between kids can become harsh and cruel in the schoolyard, the same, not surprisingly, can happen online.

» "Traditional" Bullying Versus Cyberbullying

When you think of bullying, you may think of kids on a playground picking on a peer, or a bully demanding lunch money from a younger kid. Traditional bullying often involves harassing, teasing, or forcing another kid to do something. This typically happens when the bully and victim are face to face. So what is cyberbullying? Cyberbullying is defined as using the Internet, cell phones, or social media to communicate false, embarrassing, or hostile information about someone else (Smith et al. 2008). This type of bullying can include calling someone names, spreading rumors, or making threats. It can also include pretending to be someone else online. It can involve one teen harassing another or many teens ganging up against

Table 6.1. Differences Between Cyberbullying and Bullying

Description	Cyberbullying	Bullying
General Characteristics		
Bullying takes place face-to-face and may involve physical threats		X
Bullying can happen at any time of day at any location	X	
Easy to rapidly and widely spread embarrassing information	X	
Repetitive, aggressive acts or behaviors	X	X
No direct feedback from victim	X	
Bully Characteristics		
Bully acts without regard for consequences	X	X
Bully may feel less guilty (because he or she does not have to face victim)	X	
Bully can be anonymous	X	
Bully fears punishment less	X	
Effects on Victim		
Harmful psychological effects	X	X
Anxiety and fear of encountering bully in "real life"	X	X
Risk of depression and low esteem	X	X
Fewer friends and trouble adjusting socially	X	
Enforcement		
Difficult to track down perpetrator	X	

another teen to hurt or humiliate. Table 6.1 illustrates the similarities and differences between traditional bullying and cyberbullying.

Cyberbullying may take different forms for different age groups. Tweens and early adolescents might use the Internet to insult or exclude a peer. Especially with middle adolescents, cyberbullying can become more serious and involve breaking into online accounts or stealing personal information. For example, a teen may set up a fake Facebook profile of the victim and provide false or embarrassing information on that profile. For older adolescents, cyberbullying is often associated with romantic rejection and can include unwanted sexual harassment or spreading rumors about that person.

FIGURE 6.1. Adolescents are constantly connected to the Internet, even when doing homework at a coffee shop with friends. This means cyberbullying can happen any time of the day.

Bullying can also take place in different ways based on which website or technology is being used. The various communication tools available in social media sites like Facebook unfortunately allow teens to engage in cyberbullying in multiple ways: private messages, public postings, and even through the formation of "hate" groups. Online gaming sites can promote interaction between players, but also can be a venue for bullying or harassing of players during play.

Teen Voices   **Researcher Voices**   Professional Voices   Parental Voices

A 2004 research study surveyed a group of university students to find out what, if anything, makes cyberbullying different among older adolescents compared to younger teens. Students identified several issues including unwanted sexual harassment and cyberstalking, which is a term that describes behaviors such as making repeated threats and/or harassment, the use of electronic media to make a person afraid or concerned for their safety, or stealing a person's online identity to falsify information (Finn 2004).

It is challenging to figure out how often cyberbullying takes place because of teens' reluctance to report it, and because of varying definitions of what "counts" as cyberbullying. One estimate is that about one-third of

FIGURE 6.2. Cyberbullies can have a nearly constant presence in their victim's lives, as bullying can happen via mobile devices.

young people experience cyberbullying (Lenhart 2007). Girls more often report being victims; boys more often report being bullies. Cyberbullying appears to affect those of different races and socioeconomic backgrounds pretty equally.

Teen Voices   **Researcher Voices**   Professional Voices   Parental Voices

SMAHRT recently conducted a study about cyberbullying among college students and learned some unexpected things. We asked focus groups to share their thoughts on whether cyberbullying happens at the college level, and one major finding was that students could not agree on what counted as cyberbullying. For example, a student in one group said that cyberbullying is "[anything] that makes someone else feel negative or feel worse or [any] attempt to make them feel worse than they are, than they do right now," whereas a student in another group said, "I suppose there's a difference between bullying and merely telling someone when they've been stupid." Without an agreed-upon definition of cyberbullying, it seems like students aren't sure what constitutes bullying behavior and when mean comments cross the line. This lack of definition may contribute to people's perceptions that bullying doesn't happen once you get to college.

The relationship between cyberbullying and more traditional bullying is still being researched. What has been learned so far is that in some cases, online bullying is an extension of school bullying. In other cases, cyberbullying occurs on its own. There are some important links between traditional and cyberbullying. First, traditional bullies are also more likely to be cyberbullies. Further, kids who are bullied at school are more likely to be victims of cyberbullying. So it appears that there are similar characteristics among bullies, whether they are traditional or cyberbullies, and there are similar characteristics among victims, whether they are victims of traditional bullying or cyberbullying (Li 2007).

« Consequences of Cyberbullying

Cyberbullying can actually be as harmful, if not more so than traditional bullying, because it offers the harasser the advantage of a greater sense of anonymity. This means a bully does not have to see their victim face-to-face. As a result, the bully may feel little guilt for his or her actions and can act without consequences. Traditional bullying usually takes place in

FIGURE 6.3. If your child seems upset each time she is on the computer, it may be a sign that cyberbullying is taking place.

a specific situation, such as during recess or after school. Cyberbullying, on the other hand, can happen anywhere, at any time, especially because of the rise in the use of "smart" mobile devices. This can create an endless sense of anxiety for those who are bullied—even if they are offline, they might feel almost constantly worried about what is being posted about them without their knowledge. The Internet also makes it easy for bullies to spread hurtful messages quickly and widely, increasing the victim's embarrassment.

Victims of cyberbullying and traditional bullying often share similar characteristics. For example, some research has shown that kids who are more likely to be victims of bullies often have below average or above average intelligence, have a mental or physical disability, or identify with a different sexual orientation from the bully. Victims are also more likely to be quiet, unassertive, and uncomfortable in leadership situations, and they may be just as uncomfortable standing up for themselves in the online environment.

Parents may wonder about how to recognize that their child is being cyberbullied. A common sign that your child might be being bullied is your teen's loss of interest or fear in going to school. This may mean your teen starts to skip classes, or his grades begin to drop. Your child may show symptoms of depression, such as losing appetite, having trouble with sleep (sleeping more or having trouble getting to sleep), withdrawing from friends and family, or showing stress while using the computer (see Figure 6.3). Your child may seek more alone time than usual. All of these are warning signs that something is not quite right, and that it's time for a conversation.

Ebony's Story

About 5 years ago I saw "Ebony" in the clinic. She had been referred for stomachaches that were keeping her out of school. Ebony, an 18-year-old high-school senior, had perfect attendance and stellar grades throughout high school...up to this point. In the clinic she described stomachaches that happened every day, starting when she woke up to go to school. They lasted all day until she was home from school, and she was missing school about 2 to 3 days a week for the last two months. "When did the stomachaches start?" I asked. "They started the day that my so-called friends posted a bunch of drunk photos of me on Facebook," she explained. She went on to describe that two months earlier she'd had her first experience with alcohol at a friend's house. She drank too much and passed out, and her friends took embarrassing pictures of her and posted them on Facebook. "The whole school saw them," she explained sadly. I'll always remember this case because for Ebony, her cyberbullies were her friends, and the embarrassing situation that resulted led to lost friendships along with consequences that were emotional as well as physical.

Cyberbullying presents unique challenges for adults. Since cyber-bullying occurs in the vast online community, it can be hard for parents, teachers, or law enforcement officials to stop bullies. On the other hand, cyberbullying often involves messages sent online, which can be saved and presented as evidence if needed. At the school level, the punishment of cy-berbullying behaviors is often difficult, since they're usually not occurring on school grounds, but rather, online. Some schools are changing their student policies to include any bullying behavior, on or off school grounds, as not permissible. Clearly there is much work to be done in this area.

« What Parents Can Do

Parents, you may well remember seeing or experiencing bullying in your youth. You can apply this experience, as well as the Healthy Internet Use model, when discussing cyberbullying with your own children.

< Balance

One way to approach balance in online communication is to talk with your teen about being as respectful in online communication as he is in offline, balancing the offline and online worlds. The Internet can give a feeling of being anonymous, or safe, which may prompt teens to lash out or tease more easily than they would in face-to-face conversation. You can encour-age your teen to stop and think about what he or she is communicating online and whether or not it would be something he or she would say in public or in face-to-face interactions.

Teen Voices   Researcher Voices   Professional Voices   Parental Voices

Usually you would think cyberbullying doesn't happen in college, but it does, and it occurs in ways you wouldn't usually think of. When I was sophomore in college, my friends and I went out for a drink and I had a little too much. My friends had just bought a new digital camera and while we were drinking we tested it out. The next day my friend posted some photos of our drunken experience, and more specifically one of me passed out on the ground. There were a bunch of comments on the photo saying, "ha ha ha!" and, "Wow, what a drunk!" and it really put me down. All I could think is why would someone even post this, they must have known how embarrassing it was for me. I just never thought I would be cyberbullied in such a way and by my own friends.

— Male older adolescent

Boundaries >

If you learn that your teen has been bullied, or if your child approaches you and says that a friend is being bullied, you can provide valuable guidance. Whether bullying takes place online or offline, the response is the same. The general recommendations that have been developed to address any type of bullying are as follows: The teen who is being bullied should confront the bully and ask them to stop. This can be a difficult thing for a teen to do, so a parent or friend can practice role-playing what he or she will say, and help the teen consider how the bully may react. If there is threat of physical harm, this confrontation should take place in a safe place, such as at school. If the bullying continues after this conversation, then it is time to involve an adult. At this point, you can take steps such as talking to the parent of the bully, talking to the teacher or a school administrator, or seeing the child's doctor to get additional support for the situation. You can also talk with your children about making sure that the messages they send are not interpreted as bullying by others.

Communication >

As with many other topics in this book, communication "early and often" is key. Discussions about bullying often begin in elementary school through school programs, and ideally should continue throughout adolescence. Parents can often use cues from their teens, for example "Guess what happened at school today? This one kid sent a really mean text to Cathy." These cues can be opportunities for communication about bullying and how to handle it.

 **Parents' Toolkit**

Parents, don't feel like you need to tackle the topic of bullying alone. There are many support systems in place to provide you additional information and support if you are in a situation with your child that involves cyberbullying. Many schools have bullying programs in place to help prevent and respond to situations. Talk to your pediatrician or health-care provider about your concerns; they can provide support, a listening ear, and resources.

Teen Voices   **Researcher Voices**   Professional Voices   Parental Voices

Research shows that when peers stand up to bullying or report the behavior to an adult, the bullying usually stops much more quickly than if it is ignored. Researchers in 2007 did a study about different strategies that teens use to address bullying behaviors. They found that teens use a number of approaches, including telling parents or school staff, lashing out verbally or physically at the bully or others, standing up to the bully without being physical, ignoring the bully, or treating hurtful comments as jokes. Of these varied strategies, the researchers found that telling parents, standing up to the bully, and getting help in other manners were the most effective in terms of reducing victimization. Parents can use this information in their discussions to empower their kids to feel like they have the ability to make a difference (Craig et al. 2007).

An Exercise to Try with Your Child

Try this exercise to show your child how writing mean or embarrassing comments online can hurt others. Have your child write down on a piece of paper the meanest, most cruel thing they can think of about someone they really don't like. They don't have to share it with you if they don't want to.

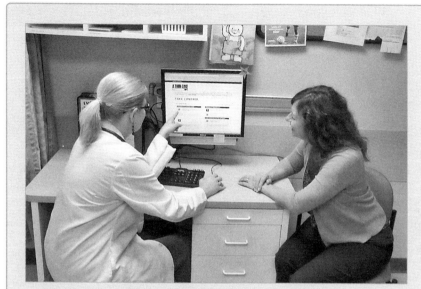

FIGURE 6.4. Talk with your child's pediatrician if you have concerns about cyberbullying.

Have them imagine saying that statement to that particular someone—*in person*. Chances are, they'll be uneasy about doing that. Then ask them if they'd be okay putting those comments on Facebook or another website for anyone to see, and what that would mean to that person as well as to your child. This exercise may help your child see that posting mean comments online can be just as hurtful as saying them in person, and may reflect poorly on your child as well.

Conversation Starters >

For the following situations about bullying, consider asking the suggested questions below. Even if you don't think that your child has experienced cyberbullying, but you are curious to know whether your child has seen these behaviors, you can ask:

- Have you ever seen any of your friends or people you know being mean to others online?
- What do you think it means to bully someone online? What might that look like?

- What have you or your friends done when others are saying mean or hurtful things online?
- What would you do if you saw someone being a bully online?

If you are concerned that your child might be a victim of cyberbullying:

- Has anything someone has said to you on the Internet ever made you feel angry, sad, or scared?
- What did they say and how did that make you feel?
- Have you talked with the person about how you felt? If so, how did it go? If not, what barriers are in the way of having this talk?
- What do you think you should do next?

If you are concerned that your child might have cyberbullied another child:

- Have you or your friends ever said anything to someone online that could have been hurtful to someone else?
- How do you think that makes the person feel?
- What made you post those hurtful comments?
- What do you think you should do next?

 This chapter's contributors included Rajitha Kota and Shari Schoohs.

7

Sex, Drugs, Rock 'n Roll— and Facebook?
Media Use and Risky Behaviors

Facebook is everywhere right now. First, the social networking site was nearly universally adopted on college campuses. Today, high schoolers everywhere also use the site to display, or "post," photos; keep friends up-to-date on daily personal developments and activities; and—post by post, picture by picture—create an online identity. Tweens get practice on Disney social networking sites that groom them for the "real world" of Facebook to come. Plenty of adults use Facebook too, with the Baby Boomers representing the fastest-growing segment of users (Minteer and Collins 2008). And let's not forget *The Social Network,* the movie made about Facebook in 2010, which garnered eight Academy Award nominations.

Social networking sites, abbreviated as SNSs, can be a fun and exciting environment for young people to forge their budding identities, but as we've touched on in earlier chapters, risks lurk there as well. For example, teens are likely to find references to drug or alcohol use or sex among their Facebook friends' posts (e.g., "got wasted last night"). These references relate to adolescent health, as substance use and risky sexual behavior are important causes of health problems among teens. Our previous research has shown high rates of these kinds of references on the Facebook profiles of older adolescents (Moreno et al. 2009). Are these posts accurate? Are they influential to others? This chapter will explore those issues. The area of social networking sites and how adolescents choose to display information about their risky health-related behaviors is a cornerstone of our research interests, so we are really excited to share the information we have learned from our past studies with you throughout this chapter. While Chapter 4 covers exposure to unwanted to inappropriate material, in this chapter we'll focus on what makes exposure to material on social media a unique area of concern.

« Social Networking 101

Yep, Facebook is the most popular of its kind today, but what we are really talking about here are traits of *all* social networking sites. Yesterday, it was MySpace; today, it's Facebook and Twitter; tomorrow, it will be…who knows? It's likely that in time a new social-networking trend will hit the scene. In fact, recent popular press coverage has indicated a movement toward smaller social networks aimed at more niche groups (Swatz 2012). New research has indicated the importance of considering these new contexts (D'Angelo et al., in press). Regardless of the size or capabilities of the SNS, young people are enjoying social networking sites, and we adults need to know a little about them to be prepared to foster healthy use and good decision-making among young people.

Living in the twenty-first century, you probably already have a good idea of what social networking sites are, but let's dig a little deeper to get even more clarity. Social networking sites are virtual communities that allow connection to others and sharing of information. Early social networking sites included MySpace: a globally accessible site designed for profile owners to share and discuss music, as well as MyYearBook: A site for high-school students to socialize and share memories. Today, the two most popular social networking sites are Facebook and Twitter. Many adolescents use social networking sites on a daily basis, and up to 97 percent of U.S. college students report ownership of a social networking site profile (Lenhart and Madden 2010). At present, the most popular SNS is Facebook, which currently boasts 130 million U.S. users and 17 billion total yearly visits (Google 2010). That's more than the population of some countries! As if that wasn't enough hype, in 2010 Facebook surpassed Google for weekly number of website hits (Childs 2010). The Facebook website states that the purpose of the website is: "*about sharing information with others—friends and people in your communities.*" Facebook's ongoing popularity may be related to its ability to combine functions such as photo sharing, e-mail communication, blogs, and RSS feeds from other sites.

FIGURE 7.1. Facebook encourages us to share and share alike.

Facebook is captivating for a lot of reasons. Teens can use Facebook to communicate with their friends, get to know acquaintances, and expand their social circle. They can express themselves online via status updates and photos, experimenting with and showcasing their new identities as they transform and develop. They can invite friends to events, and create groups of like-minded people.

Key features of Facebook include:

Creation of a personal web profile: The personal web profile is a showcase of the profile owner's identity. Profile content is created and displayed by the profile owner and may include audio, images (e.g., pictures and video), and text (e.g., blogs and personal descriptions). A widely used feature of some SNSs such as Facebook is called "status updates," which allow users to share a short text description of their current location, emotion, or activity. Examples of status updates include: "Jeff is feeling pretty tired" or "Erika got good news today!" SNSs often allow profile owners to create online photo albums and to share photographs with other profile owners.

Communication: SNSs also provide a venue for communication with other profile owners via e-mail, instant messaging, and publicly displayed comments.

Networking: SNSs provide opportunities to link one's profile into a social network via "friending." When two profile owners accept each other as online "friends" the two profiles become linked and content is mutually accessible. Profile owners can also create "groups" which are either publicly or privately available groups of networked profiles. Groups can include high school clubs, campus organizations, or even students in an academic class.

Event planning: Facebook allows profile owners to display events on the profile, invite others within Facebook to attend the events, and track who is planning to attend.

Facebook and Privacy

One of the big issues with Facebook is privacy. Who actually gets to see what young people are posting on their Facebook pages? And how good is Facebook, the company, at keeping young people's personal information safe?

Parents have likely heard reports in the news about Facebook and privacy concerns. Media reports have highlighted how Facebook has changed their privacy settings several times, leading to confusion among profile owners about how to keep their information protected.

Let's look at a quick history of privacy on Facebook. This particular social networking site allows profile owners to establish settings for how their information is shared with other Facebook users. These profile security settings have evolved several times over the past few years, and it's hard for most of us to keep up. Early on, profile owners could choose to make all profile content "public," or available to all other Facebook users, or "private" and only available to other profile owners who were Facebook friends. Now, settings include several security options that can be customized to different sections of the profile or for different Facebook friends. For example, if you are friends with your child on Facebook, she can provide you access to some online albums of photographs but block other online albums from your view. As a viewer of another person's profile, you typically can only view content that that profile owner has *allowed* you to access, and you cannot tell whether or how much content has been hidden.

If you are concerned about what your kids may be posting for their friends on Facebook, finding out that information is an important place to start. But you may also want to look deeper. As adults, we have to keep an eye on what Facebook, *the company,* is doing with young people's information too.

You may remember when Facebook shifted its privacy practices in 2009. Without getting users' consent or giving a warning, the company made users' private profile information public. So if Sarah bought Sam a book as a holiday gift on a shopping website, that information was made available to Sam via Facebook. (Scary!) As if it wasn't enough that young people needed to learn to discern what information was appropriate to share with designated friends on Facebook, suddenly their private posts to individual friends, photos, and shopping choices could be read by anyone surfing the Web.

After much media hype and public push-back, Facebook adjusted its policies to better protect the consumer. In addition, the FTC ruled in November of 2011 that Facebook was out of compliance with the 2009 actions, rendering the corporation subject to regular privacy audits for the next twenty years (Collins, Kashdan, and Gollnisch 2003). This example stands as a reminder that it's important to be aware of not just what other friends may learn about our kids on Facebook but also how the company handles its users' information.

Facebook Advertisements >

How does Facebook use young people's personal information when it comes to advertisers? If you've ever spent any time on Facebook yourself, then you know that advertisements are frequent on Facebook. What you may or may not know is that these advertisements are directly targeted to content that is displayed on a user's Facebook page. I know of one 50-something woman who lamented the advertisement of a snoring aid (CPAP machine) on her Facebook page! Now let's look at how this might apply to young people. If your child plays soccer, it's likely that displaying keywords such as "soccer" on his profile will trigger advertisements for soccer equipment.

FIGURE 7.2. Facebook is becoming a popular way for companies to spread the word about the products and services they provide.

Teen Voices   **Researcher Voices**   Professional Voices   Parental Voices

In a recent study we evaluated advertisements on Facebook that were shown when profile owners wrote status updates about dieting or fitness. We found that most information on advertisements were of poor quality (diets such as the "Oreo Cookie Diet" or "Fat burning furnace"). One concerning finding in this research study was that after posting a status update about being too thin and needing to gain some weight, the advertisements that appeared were for weight-loss diets. This research study shows that Facebook advertisements are triggered to keywords on the profile but may not always show accurate or appropriate content. That's a concern for those of us who care about surrounding young people with positive media influence (Villiard and Moreno 2012).

Any discussion of social networking wouldn't be complete without mentioning Twitter. Twitter shares some similarities with Facebook, but there are also differences between the two. Twitter developed as a micro-blogging site in which short sequences of text (usually 140 characters) are displayed publicly. These micro blogs, or "tweets," are shared with users in an ongoing, continuously updated RSS feed. Similar to Facebook, Twitter users create a profile that includes a user name and password. In contrast to Facebook, though, there is more emphasis on output via "tweets" than in a multimedia identity creation.

While young people are busy tweeting cool links and news flashes to their followers and the overall Twittersphere, some adults are still trying to figure out the verb form of posting on this particular social networking site. Are kids "twittering"? or "tweetering"? If you know much about Twitter, then you know they are in fact "tweeting"—sending out messages to anyone who "follows" them online, meaning anyone who reads their tweets.

An added challenge to this communication is that tweets are limited to 140 characters at a time. (It is safe to say our teens today are learning about brevity from social media!) On its website, Twitter states its goal "is to provide a service that allows you to discover and receive content from sources that interest you as well as to share your content with others." No invitation or special friend designation is needed; Twitter is by default public—anyone can choose to "follow" anyone else.

We know much less about the risks and benefits of Twitter among teens, as its popularity

FIGURE 7.3. Twitter is another way for adolescents to communicate with one another online. It is important that they understand how to use the site safely, such as by avoiding tweeting personal information.

among teens is much more recent (Litt and Stock 2011). It's reasonable to consider that the more personal the information a teen chooses to display publicly, the more risks that may be present if that information is passed along to the wrong person, or to too many people! Since Twitter profiles typically display less personal information compared to Facebook, there may be lower risks, but there is still much to learn about this social networking site.

« Benefits and Risks of Social Networking Sites

Social networking sites, like any other form of media, are tools that present both potential benefits as well as potential risks for young people. For teens who feel isolated, such as adolescents with interests that are unusual in their home community, sites like Facebook and Twitter may provide a social outlet that is otherwise difficult to reach. As noted in Chapter 1, a research study found a relationship between positive self-esteem and satisfaction

FIGURE 7.4. Facebook's event function lets you invite people to events and allows people to RSVP directly to the invitation on Facebook.

with Facebook use (Ellison, Steinfield, and Lampe 2007). Anecdotal reports suggest that some adolescents use social networking sites to organize potentially beneficial activities through the "events" function, such as class assignments, social justice efforts, or support groups for peers in distress. We've seen teens use Facebook to share ideas on an upcoming presidential election or to organize a special gathering to support a friend whose parent recently died.

Despite these potential benefits, there may be risks associated with the content that a young person posts on their Facebook page. For example, if the young person displays information about drinking alcohol on his profile—what clinicians would call a "health-risk behavior"—this information is now posted in a globally public venue. Remember, content displayed on a Facebook profile can be copied and saved, downloaded, or distributed by any profile viewer. As a result, this information is: published, public, permanent, and persuasive.

What's more, as many adolescents link their Facebook profiles to large numbers of friends, it can be challenging for teens to understand the reach of the information they are displaying and to make appropriate decisions given such a widespread reach. As one parent described to us in a focus group:

> I was floored when we were having this discussion and somebody was telling me about their child who has a Twitter account and has five hundred people follow him. I thought, really? You know we are talking a high-school-age youth. Five hundred people following him. And again I don't think they understand or have any idea what that means.

This information may then become accessible to people whom the young person would prefer not to view it, such as school bullies, teachers, and of course potential employers. As we've seen in the news, many employers currently screen potential job candidates using websites like Facebook (Kluemper and Rosen 2009). Considering these benefits and risks can help frame our next topic about teens displaying information about health behaviors on SNSs.

« Adolescents' Health Displays on Social Networking Sites

A major need (or developmental task) of adolescents is to develop their identity; social networking sites provide them a technological venue for the exploration of who they are or want to be. This exploration may include references to favorite movies, recent events, hobbies, or experiences. Through developing and updating a social networking profile, adolescents choose what parts of their identity to display, and at what times. Adolescents often receive feedback from peers on these displays via publicly posted comments on their profile, which may influence their views or behaviors both online and offline. For example, an adolescent who posts a reference to a new song she heard, and then gets a lot of positive comments from friends on her Facebook profile, may end up wanting to buy more music by that artist.

Adolescence is frequently a time of behavioral experimentation. For some adolescents, this includes experimenting with risky behaviors like drinking alcohol (Neinstein and Anderson 2002). These health-risk behaviors may also become part of the displayed identity that adolescents present on their social networking profiles. In several previous studies of these profiles, about half of adolescent social networking profiles showed references to one or more health-risk behaviors (Moreno, Parks, and Richardson 2007; Hinduja and Patchin 2008; Moreno et al. 2009). One of our early studies on SNSs found that approximately 41 percent of older adolescents' profiles displayed references (posts) to substance use, 24 percent displayed references to sex, and 14 percent displayed references to violence (Moreno et al. 2009). Given that most profiles contain information that clearly identifies the profile owner, posts about these types of behaviors are particularly problematic. Especially so, as revealing risky material online may be more likely to attract unwanted attention from a cyberbully or predator. Linking that information to your child's identity including home address or school is quite worrisome.

When considering these social networking displays, two questions are essential for you as parents to consider. First, what is the accuracy of the information presented by the adolescent profile owner? This is important to consider so that you can determine how to approach this information if you see it on your child's profile. Second, regardless of the accuracy of the displayed information, what is the possible impact on your child who views the social networking profiles of peers who post problematic information?

Are Social Networking Displays Accurate? >

Consider this potential real-life scenario. A 16-year-old male writes on his Facebook profile: "My favorite beer is Bud Light!" There are several possibilities of what this display, usually in the form of a post, may mean. It's possible that the teen is writing this comment to show people that he drinks beer. On the other hand, this posted display could also mean that the teen is *considering* trying alcohol and wants to "try on" the identity of a drinker first to see what sort of response is triggered among his peers. These types of displays could also be jokes or nonsense.

A first clue to these displays can be found in psychological and computer science studies. These studies have shown that computer use encourages high levels of self-disclosure and "uninhibited personal expression." This finding suggests that the online environment may encourage one to discuss or reveal personal information (Fleming 1990; Newman et al. 1997; Walther and Parks 2002; Wallace et al. 2006). Further, people who tend to disclose personal information in *offline* environments are also are more likely to disclose personal information in *online* environments (Christofides, Muise, and Desmarais 2009). So if a young person is talkative and comfortable sharing about herself at school, she may also be more likely to disclose information about herself on Facebook. Makes sense.

Second, it is worth considering a theory known as the Media Practice Model. This model identifies key factors in adolescents' use of media and argues that adolescents select and interact with media based on who they are—or who they want to be—at the moment. The model supports that what young people choose to display on the Internet may reflect actual behaviors *or* behavioral intent (Brown 2000).

Third, patterns of posted information on SNSs may also give clues to whether the displayed information is likely to be closer to the truth or far from it. Some of our early research showed that references to risky behaviors on SNS profiles are often displayed in patterns consistent with those seen in research studies that asked teens about these same behaviors (Moreno, Parks, and Richardson 2009). For example, SNS profiles that display references to one risk behavior, such as substance use, are more likely to display references to other risk behaviors, such as sex. Similarly, in many past research studies, teens who answered a survey question that they had drunk alcohol were also more likely to disclose that they had had sex. Our past research also found that references to health-risk behaviors that appear on a teenager's profile are also displayed in similar patterns among that teenager's online "friend" groups (Moreno et al. 2010). Numerous previous studies have also found that teens often engage in similar risk behaviors that their peers are doing. This is probably consistent with every parent's instincts. If you find out your child is hanging out with a group of teens who smoke, you are probably a lot more worried about your child taking up smoking. Thus, if you notice your child's friends on Facebook are posting about alcohol use, it's time to ask your child some questions about his or her own alcohol attitudes and behavior.

Finally, more recent research has directly investigated links between online displays and offline disclosures. In a recent research study of college students from two universities, we evaluated Facebook profiles for evidence of alcohol use in either status updates or photographs. Profiles were categorized as "Intoxication/Problem Drinking Displayers" if the profile owner discussed getting drunk or engaging in problem drinking behaviors such as driving drunk or passing out. Profiles were considered "Alcohol Displayers" if alcohol was referenced but no intoxication or problem drinking was noted. Profiles were considered "Non-Displayers" if no alcohol was present. We found that college students who chose to post references to intoxication or problem drinking on Facebook were more likely to meet problem-drinking criteria (using a clinical screening survey) compared to participants who were Alcohol Displayers or Non-Displayers. Parents can take away from this finding that references to "getting wasted" or "can't remember last night" on a teen or college student's social networking site profile suggest a higher likelihood that alcohol abuse may be taking place and that it is time for a conversation (Moreno et al. 2012).

Are These Social Networking Posts Influential to Adolescents? >

A model parent, Jorge has reviewed all of his teenage son Jack's Facebook posts and pictures. He is pleased that Jack has not posted any comments about alcohol or other risky behaviors. He notices that a few of Jack's friends are not so careful with their Facebook profiles and post about things like wanting to "party and get drunk." Jorge may wonder, "Should I care about these posts? They're not on Jack's profile. Could this information affect him?" In considering this scenario, parents may remember their own adolescent years and how much their peer's attitudes impacted them. Peer influence is one of the strongest sources of influence among adolescents, particularly adolescents in the high-school years. During middle adolescence, teens commonly adopt the attitudes, intentions, and behaviors of their main peer group. This influence can attract teens to participating in behaviors they would have never considered in younger years. As one parent described to us during a focus-group study:

> Peer pressure is serious. A teen says, "Sure I drink alcohol or I'm sexually active," and all of the sudden there's this peer pressure that might not even be legitimate. And [for a teen] everything is piling on and there's this sense that because everyone seems to be doing it that it's okay. But who knows, you can't really verify that information or know that it is true.

In the online world, teens can be exposed to health-risk behaviors on the social networking profiles of peers. It is important to remember that social networking data is both created and consumed by adolescents. Thus, it combines both media influence *and* peer influence! Regardless of the accuracy of what is on Facebook, other adolescents may respond to a peer's Facebook disclosures as if they were real, and this in turn may influence the teen's intentions and behaviors. Our previous study found that adolescents viewed alcohol references on social networking profiles as both accurate *and* influential representations of alcohol use (Moreno et al. 2009).

There are several theories that have contributed to our understanding of how this presumption may happen. Given the popularity of social networking sites, these websites may function as a media "superpeer," promoting and establishing norms of behavior among other adolescents (Strasburger and Wilson 2002). Because most displayed content about alcohol use on social media presents alcohol in a positive light as fun and social and without risk, these alcohol references on social networking sites may promote the illusion that drinking is safe and fun. These posts may influence teens to think alcohol use is normal and fun and may promote alcohol initiation, a process known as media cultivation (Gerbner et al. 1986).

Social learning theory predicts that teens who see a media figure, such as a television celebrity, engaging in behaviors such as alcohol use without experiencing negative consequences will be more likely to try the behaviors themselves (Bandura 1977; Bandura 1986). This makes some intuitive sense. If a child watches a TV show where someone touches a hot stove and cries out in pain, that child will probably remember not to touch hot stoves. But if the stove was touched without any bad consequences, that child will likely try it herself. Though this example is pretty simplistic, a great deal of research supports that similar patterns of observation and behavior occur with teens as they observe behaviors on television, movies, Facebook, and of course in offline life too. Here are some examples of past studies that have shown the power of media influence:

A study by Robinson and colleagues looked at 9th grade students and whether media use was associated with alcohol use. They found that increased time spent watching any type of television or movie was associated with a high risk of starting to use alcohol among students who hadn't drunk before (Robinson, Chen, and Killin 1998).

One research study examined the relationship between television watching and smoking. Researchers found that youth who watched excessive television, 5 or more hours per day, were about six times more likely to start smoking cigarettes (Gidwani et al. 2002)!

A study by Dr. Sarah Ashby, a pediatrician, looked at groups of adolescents who reported that their parents disapproved of them having sex. Among this group of teens, those who watched two hours of television a day or more were more likely to start having sex early compared to teens who didn't watch this much television (Ashby, Arcari, and Edmonson 2006).

Most of these studies focus on younger teens and older forms of media such as television. Newer research has indicated that adolescents and college students often use social networks to find out information about new friends (Courtois 2012). The idea of adolescents using Facebook to seek information from each other is thought to be a powerful form of influence that has been called "interpersonal persuasion." The power of interpersonal persuasion cannot be underestimated among adolescents and young adults, for whom peers are the most important source of influence. Facebook provides a venue for peer interaction and social networking; both are recognized as contributors to behaviors such as substance use. Facebook has been described as "the most significant advance in persuasion since the radio was invented in the 1890s" and initiated a new form of persuasion labeled "mass interpersonal persuasion" (Fogg 2008).

| Teen Voices | **Researcher Voices** | Professional Voices | Parental Voices |

One unique element of Facebook is simply how much information is on it: You can learn a lot of information about a person from their pictures, self-disclosures in an "about me" section, and in public comments from their friends, or wall posts. Given the vast amount of information available, research has considered what type of information matters the most when forming a first impression of an individual and deciding how to interact with them. A past research study found that when looking at a profile and judging its owner, the things that other people write about the profile owner (wall posts) were most likely to influence a viewer, followed by photographs of the profile owner. Written statements in the "about me" section matter the least. This is thought to be the case because while written statements can be easy to fake, it is harder to fake photographs and even harder fake or manipulate wall posts written by other people (Walther 2012). Thus, when you consider both your child's profile and those of their friends, keep a keen eye on the wall posts and photos—this is the information that research suggests will be the most influential to profile viewers.

As for college students, students have told our research group that the transition to college is frequently a time in which students will seek

Teen Voices | Researcher Voices | **Professional Voices** | Parental Voices

I recently worked on a study in which we presented soon-to-be college students a scenario where they were shown the Facebook profile of a new friend who had invited them to a party. We asked them how likely they would be to drink with this new friend at the party. We found that when the new friend had a profile characterized by references to drinking, adolescents were LESS likely to want to drink with this new friend, whereas when the friend's profile was characterized by "responsible" posts (in this case wall posts about study groups) adolescents were actually more likely to drink with this new friend! In interviews, adolescents explained this trend by indicating that they would rather drink with someone who appeared responsible, as opposed to someone who posted about drinking in an inappropriate way, which made them look irresponsible. This illustrates that teens use Facebook information as a way to create impressions about new friends and make decisions about what behaviors they are willing to engage in with that new friend.

— Male graduate student

information on Facebook about students at the school they plan to attend. If alcohol is frequently displayed on Facebook profiles, this can give the impression that alcohol is part of the social norm of college at that school. This can lead a future college student to believe that it is an expectation that alcohol will play a large role in college life and could limit them in learning about all that college has to offer.

≪ What Parents Can Do

Because social networking sites have only been around for the last decade, some parents may feel uneasy about providing guidance to their teens regarding how to use these sites. However, in the sections below we'll include tips from the Healthy Internet Use Model to illustrate that parents can stick to the lessons and advice they know best, even when discussing the newest social media site.

Balance >

In the past, people would talk about the balance between online life and "real life." However, as several teens have said to me in clinic: "My online life is a big part of my real life, not something separate from it!" It seems true that for teens today, the distinction lies between their online and offline lives as integrated parts of their real lives. As a parent, your job is to help your child find a healthy balance between the offline and online worlds in which they navigate each day. This may include encouraging your child to hang out with a friend in person rather than texting all night from home.

Boundaries >

Boundaries on SNSs are key; these include boundaries about whom your child should and should not interact with or "friend," as well as boundaries around what type of information your child should and should not post online. As a parent you'll also want to consider the boundaries between you and your child about what you can and cannot view. For younger teens, many parents make rules about transparency to be sure they know what is posted and who can see it. As teens get older and demonstrate safe behaviors, many parents are able to let go of some of the earlier rules. The following is advice from a parent about setting boundaries:

> We have ALL website/computer/iPod passwords for our kids' e-mail and Facebooks. I am my son's "friend" on Facebook as well and have been quite happy that several of his friends have "friended" me— keeps me in the loop without having to feel like I'm snooping. That being said, I do log on to his Facebook account now and then to make sure things look all right and to check who he messages with. My son and I have conversations about what might or might not be a good thing to post, talk about the crazy things others say and do on Facebook. I am quick to let him know that adults make bad choices as well and that sometimes less is more! The biggest difference I notice between my generation and his on Facebook is that he is friends with people he barely knows. People that he wouldn't have a real conversation with but that go to his school or know friends

of his. It's interesting to me how these people learn so much about each other without really even knowing one another. I think it gives them a sense of feeling connected to other teens.

Communication

Communication regarding social networking sites is easy to prompt—just look at the newspaper and there is likely to be a story about Facebook or Twitter. Some parents may feel nervous that their teen knows more about this site than they do, and it is ok to let them take the lead as the teen expert on Facebook use and you take the lead on Internet safety. Frequent communication at the start of social-networking-site use is key, and this frequency may naturally decrease over time…or it could remain a topic of conversation as a way to stay connected to your child and what he is interested in as he becomes an older adolescent.

Teen Voices   Researcher Voices   Professional Voices   Parental Voices

We talked about it when I first signed up for Facebook—about not being friends with people who I don't know and posting bad stuff, but we don't really talk about it so much anymore. I know what the rules are though, and I know if I break the big rules like looking at something inappropriate that I'll lose my privileges.

— Male younger adolescent

 **Parents' Toolkit**

Here are a few key considerations for parents in providing their children with guidance for safe SNS use:

1. Let's get back to our 16-year-old teen who displayed his fondness for Bud Light on Facebook. What can parents do when they notice this status update? This situation presents an incredible opportunity to discuss both online safety and family rules about alcohol use. While we have considered in this chapter whether or not posts about sex, alcohol, or drugs on Facebook are accurate, *any* disclosure of a health-risk behavior

on your child's profile is worth discussing. Even if you believe "my child would never do that!" it is still worth talking with your child about how that type of self-presentation may impact him or influence what others think about who he is.

One way to start the discussion is to point out to your child that you saw the post or photo on Facebook. Since discussions about alcohol can be difficult, beginning with a fact, such as what was published on his or her Facebook page, can be easier than trying to start the conversation about alcohol use in vague or accusatory terms.

Recently we did a research study to find out ways adolescents would like to be approached if an alcohol display were seen on their profile. These older adolescents explained that they would want to be approached privately and with questions such as, "I saw this on your profile, can you tell me about it?" rather than with immediate judgments about what the display may mean. Finally, they stated that being reminded of how that person cares for them would help make the conversation less awkward. One example would be: "I realize that you need independence in how you use Facebook, but I want to talk with you about this because I really care about you and your health" (Moreno et al. 2012).

The disclosure of substance use may represent actual behavior or behavioral intent. In either case, it is time to talk with your child about his attitudes and intentions about alcohol use. If he has not yet drunk alcohol, what motivated him to post about beer? Does he feel peer pressure to display this? If so, why? If he has drunk alcohol, it is time to discuss or reinforce family rules about alcohol use.

2. Once in awhile, view a profile of a friend of your child together with your child. Discuss different information that is displayed and ask your child what information you think is safe or unsafe. Consider starting the conversation with something like: "I saw that your friend posted on Facebook about drinking a lot of beer. Let's talk about this. What do you think about this type of post?" As one parent explained to us, using the profile of a peer, rather than the profile of one's own child as an example can help the conversation focus more on safety and less on defensiveness. During a focus group, a teacher discussed her recommendation

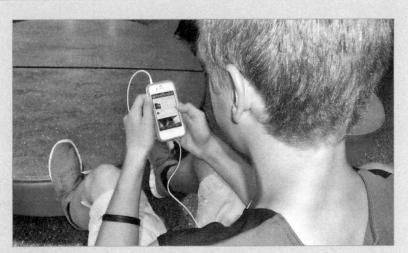

FIGURE 7.5. Posting here, there, and everywhere. It is common for teens to use cell phones and iPods to post on Facebook, Twitter, and other social networking sites.

that parents frequently view profiles of peers: "When they pull up their friend's Facebook page or something like that, then they can pick out, yeah, this shouldn't be there, this shouldn't be there. This should be here. And then when they finally look at their [own profile], I think it makes a little bit more sense."

« Beyond Facebook

Facebook is clearly the hot thing today and may or may not continue as such. In this chapter we have tried to focus on the underlying aspects of Facebook that provide both benefits and risks to today's youth. Creating and presenting an online identity, networking with friends, and communication are all key elements of social media. An understanding of these fundamentals can help you, as the parent or caring adult, to consider what these sites offer to kids and ways to help advise them in staying safe.

 This chapter's contributors included Jon D'Angelo, Kaitlyn Bare, and Suzanne Murray.

8

Addicted to the Internet?
Considering Problematic Internet Use (PIU)

Today, addiction to alcohol, drugs, gambling, and even sex are considered medical conditions requiring intervention and support. Can addiction to the Internet also occur? And if so how are young people at risk? In recent years, concerns regarding Internet addiction have arisen, with researchers

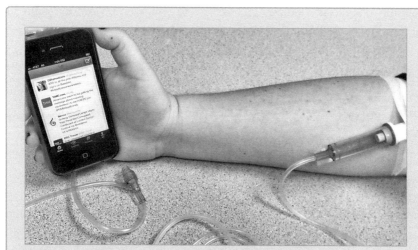

FIGURE 8.1. Does it seem like some teens need a constant infusion of the Internet?

discovering that certain types or amounts of online use may be potentially "harmful" or "problematic." While many terms have been used to describe problematic Internet use, including "Internet addiction," for this chapter we'll stick to the more broad term of problematic Internet use, abbreviated PIU.

The idea of Internet overuse may not be surprising given that over the past decade, Internet use has grown in both its reach across the youth population and the depth to which it is integrated into young people's lives. Youth spend hours a day online, and the number of hours per day has greatly increased over the last decade. The availability of smartphones makes this access easier than ever before. Young people may log onto the Internet literally dozens of times a day, or have a constant online presence in their background, with frequent checks for new information and activity.

What is problematic Internet use, and how often does it happen? It is difficult to know for sure how often PIU occurs because of the lack of consensus on what it actually is. Our group recently conducted a research study using a screening test for Internet addiction called the Young Internet Addiction Test. We found that about 4 percent of older adolescents screened as "at risk for" Internet addiction (Christakis et al. 2011). However, it is a little difficult to know what those findings mean because this particular measurement scale is a bit old, having been created in the late 1990s. It includes questions such as, "How often do you spend too much time in chat rooms?" which most teens today would probably answer with a firm "NEVER." There are many scales to measure PIU, and few of them have had good research studies to support their use. This may help explain the broad ranges that studies have shown, as previous studies have reported rates of PIU anywhere between 0 percent up to 25 percent of teens (Moreno et al. 2011).

« Problematic Internet Use: Defining the Problem

Interest in the idea of problematic Internet use has grown in the past decade among parents, teachers, and psychiatrists. The major psychiatry textbook used in the United States, the *Diagnostic and Statistical Manual of Mental Disorders-V*, includes a mention of Internet addiction, calling it a "disorder

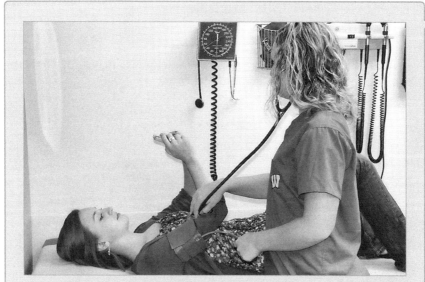

FIGURE 8.2. An overly connected teen patient uses her phone during her annual checkup. Is this PIU?

in need of further study." This statement gets at the heart of a major issue with problematic Internet use—how to define PIU. This difficulty with definition is likely related to the varied approaches that have been taken by different groups who research it.

When researchers and clinicians first started studying problematic Internet use, some assumed it would be a disorder similar to other "behavioral" addictions like shopping or gambling. In fact, some research studies took existing clinical criteria for addictions like gambling and just substituted the word "Internet" for "gambling." Other research groups have assumed that Internet addiction is similar to a substance-use addiction, such as alcohol or drugs. Still other groups have used different psychological approaches toward defining and measuring this problem. The problem is that many of the clinical screening scales that have been developed as a result of these approaches just don't work in clinical practice, perhaps because the scales were designed for another disorder. Our recent research study evaluated one of the commonly used screens and found that it did not perform well in a study of older adolescents, either statistically or practically (Jelenchick et al. 2011).

« A Framework for Understanding Problematic Internet Use

When our research team began looking into problematic Internet use, we felt that one key piece of information was missing: the perspectives of adolescents themselves on what they felt defined problematic Internet use. We as adults may *think* we know what PIU is, but because adolescents are considered by many to be the most high-risk group for PIU, our team was really curious to learn what adolescents felt made up this disorder. We spent a year studying their views and experiences, as well as the views of health-care providers who care for teens specifically, to develop a comprehensive view of PIU. We found a great deal of overlap between what adolescents and clinicians, including nurses, physicians, and counselors, considered to be PIU.

< *Symptom Categories*

The findings from this research study suggest that the following general categories of symptoms make up PIU for adolescents and young adults:

Physical Impairment
Weight gain, vision changes, and sore back or wrists are all symptoms of Internet overuse that teens have described to us. Feeling tired due to late-night log-ons is also a common sign of overuse.

Internet Use Dependency
Feeling irritated or angry are the most commonly described symptoms in our studies. These symptoms are experienced when the teen is away from the Internet and wants to get back to it.

Impulsive Internet Use
Symptoms relate to a lack of control associated with being online, either having trouble getting themselves to log off, or having trouble getting other things done without going back to the Internet for a quick log-on. Specific signs of impulsive use include letting the Internet get in the way of important, everyday activities, or avoiding activities in order to stay online, or using the Internet to avoid homework or tasks.

Risky Internet Use

Risky Internet use has not been described in previous measurement tools for Internet addiction, but it is a behavior that we hear about frequently in our research studies as well as in clinic. Risky use includes using the Internet to access inappropriate information, such as pornography or violent material. The user may know that this information is inappropriate but seek it out anyway.

Social/Functional Impairment

Symptoms of social or functional impairment may occur from being online too much or accessing inappropriate material online. These symptoms include decreases in grades or skipping class to stay on the Internet, avoiding offline social events to stay online, and preferring to socialize online instead of offline.

How Teens View PIU >

When we asked teens about their views on PIU and whether they saw extended time on the Internet as a problem, we got some insightful examples. Some quotes from teens in our research studies include:

> I think [PIU] definitely becomes an issue when it affects productivity and whether you get what you need to done and becomes an issue when you are using it for other reasons than you should be.
>
> — Female adolescent

> Maybe like the illegal stuff too. I guess if you're doing illegal activity that's more problematic. It's another dimension that makes it even more complicated. Like it's not as bad as stealing money to check e-mail too much…but still an issue.
>
> — Male adolescent

One teen brought up the difficulty in the large "gray zone" that could make up an area between normal and problematic Internet use. She suggested that it could be challenging to determine if something "is really a problem or more of a habit that might be annoying to some people or is it really destructive?"

Our study clearly cannot solve all of the potential gray areas in PIU, but we felt like it was an important step toward a more comprehensive view of what may make up PIU in adolescents.

Measuring Problematic Internet Use

A major barrier to the identification of PIU among adolescents is a lack of a cohesive screening tool. Doctors and nurses often use screening tools to identify depression, anxiety, and other health concerns. To be useful, the tool needs to be reliable and get the same result with the same person even if it is given more than once. It also needs to be accurate, and measure what it is designed to measure. The screening tool must also be valid, and reflect one illness rather than a bunch of random symptoms. As you can imagine, designing such a screening tool is not easy.

We were interested in how clinicians and parents could determine whether an adolescent or young adult may have PIU and led a study to develop a screening test. As soon as this screening instrument has been fully scientifically evaluated, we hope to release it for use in clinician offices. Stay tuned!

Ages and Stages and PIU

How may PIU vary across ages and stages of adolescence? Not much is known about PIU, so we'll give some potential examples that come from clinical and research experience. We will keep our examples broad to protect the identity of the teens we describe.

One way that PIU may begin is with online gaming among younger teens. Young teens may initially start playing online games as entertainment or distraction, but get wrapped up in the risk-reward associated with the games as well as the social circle that can be created by interacting with other online gamers. A teen may spend increasing amounts of time alone in his room playing online games. One parent described a teen who would only come out of his room to get food or go to the bathroom, then it was back in again with door shut. Gaming in and of itself is not a bad thing, but if pursued in excess, and at expense of other offline social experiences, this can be a problem.

Middle adolescents may continue patterns from early adolescence if the patterns are not detected and remedied, but middle adolescents may also get swept up in their new access to online social networks. For some adolescents with social anxiety or depression or isolation, these online social interactions may feel safer to them than offline social interactions. One teen may have had trouble in elementary school making friends, so when she found a group of friends on Facebook during middle school her mom was thrilled. When she started skipping church events to stay on Facebook chat, her mom grew concerned that she was missing out on opportunities to make friends in her youth group. If your middle adolescent is skipping offline social events such as parties to stay online, this may be a sign that your teen is a bit too reliant on the Internet for socialization. A teen in one of our research studies explained: "I would say a lot in adolescence, social problems develop in [the] school setting so you turn to [the] Internet to try and relieve pain or whatever or make up for social aspects you're missing, so then you develop dependence on it."

Older adolescents may run into challenges with having so much unregulated time on their hands once they have moved out of their parents' homes. What was a fun distraction online, such as shopping or music sharing or gaming, could become an impulsive behavior and lead to PIU.

FIGURE 8.3. Teens can sometimes use the Internet so much that it may interfere with daily everyday activities.

One college student described spending literally days in his dorm room playing online games and skipping classes. Without some external push to go out and socialize, he was missing out on all that college had to offer.

« Negative Consequences of Problematic Internet Use

The cases above illustrate potential negative consequences associated with PIU. Several research studies have also shown negative consequences associated with PIU. These can include negative health consequences such as increased risk of depression symptoms, ADHD symptoms, excessive daytime sleepiness, even increased risk for problematic alcohol use. PIU has also been associated with missing classes and negative academic consequences such as lower grades and even academic dismissal. Perhaps most serious are the case reports from Asia in which young adults have died. One media story described a young man who spent over 50 hours in an Internet café and then had a heart attack (Christakis 2010).

Many parents know all too well the negative consequences of excessive Internet use—the teen who won't come out of their bedroom for hours on a weekend or the teen who falls asleep during breakfast because of a late night on the computer. Some parents may also know of the negative consequences of risky Internet use, such as looking at dangerous material discussed in Chapter 4.

« What Parents and Professionals Can Do

There is still a lot to discover about PIU and how to prevent, identify, and treat it among adolescents. Even so, there are ways that parents and professionals can work with adolescents to prevent the development of PIU through the Healthy Internet Use model.

< The Role of Parents

The key issue with potential PIU arises around balance, as the concern is often that the teen is spending too much time online and has thus developed an inappropriate attachment to being online.

FIGURE 8.4. An adolescent and her mom take a moment to check in on her Internet use patterns. These discussions don't have to be serious and long; they can be frequent, quick check-ins.

| Teen Voices | Researcher Voices | Professional Voices | **Parental Voices** |

We keep the computer in a central location in the house. Our kids don't have laptops (yet) so we have been able to keep pretty good tabs on what websites they are accessing, etc., because it is all on the same computer, in the middle of our busy house. Part of the reason we have not gotten our teenager his own laptop is that I don't want him up in his room on the Internet all the time—for safety and just because it's such a time "zapper." We might never see him!!!

— Female parent

Boundaries may also be an issue with PIU, as the teen may be engaging with content that is risky or inappropriate.

The key to addressing these concerns lies in communication. Some conversation starters are listed below in the toolkit.

A Role for Health Professionals and Teachers

Many guidelines suggest bringing your child to a health professional if you are worried about PIU. In fact, some physicians screen for Internet use and media use at each visit. This approach is even recommended by the American Academy of Pediatrics. In one of our research projects we asked older adolescents if they would be ok with being screened for problematic Internet use at the doctor's office, and this is what we heard:

> I think this is definitely something you could ask at a yearly checkup. It could be grouped with alcohol, tobacco, or even seatbelt use questions. You wouldn't expect it coming from them, but it could definitely fit in.
>
> — Female adolescent

> It wouldn't hurt to ask at all, hard to tell just by asking, because some kids tend to lie but if they admit to it, then doctors can help them.
>
> — Male adolescent

One teen described an approach on how to educate, prevent, and treat PIU:

> If kids were educated about it by parents or teachers at a younger age then [they] could recognize it when they got older, like drugs and stuff. Then seek out support on their own or [in an] Internet support group...I could totally see that happening.
>
> — Male adolescent

Other teens discussed the role that teachers could play in educating students about problematic Internet use so that today's teens can try to avoid PIU, or at least recognize early signs of it. One teen explained:

> It would be a good idea for teachers, while they're pushing technology-based education styles, then it'd be a good time to address overuse concerns of the Internet. We talked about issues with depression and things in school, but not how it's connected to Internet use.
>
> — Female adolescent

Parents' Toolkit

Here are some conversation starters that you as parents can use if you are concerned about problematic Internet use.

- Look, I know that it is normal for teens your age to be online a lot. But I've noticed in the past few months that you are spending increasing hours in your room alone on the computer. This has me worried. I don't want you to miss out on all the other things out there that the world has to offer you. There is something called problematic Internet use, which is when someone uses the Internet too much or has an inappropriate attachment to being on the Internet. Given what I've just told you, do you think we should be worried about your Internet use?

- I've noticed that you've been on the Internet more than you used to be, and last week I noticed that you skipped Pete's party to stay online. Do you sometimes feel like it is easier for you to socialize online than in person?

- Last week I asked you to get off the computer to come to a family dinner and you seemed really angry. Can you tell me about what made you angry? Were you mad at your sister or were you missing the experience of being online? What do you think it means if you were missing the Internet during the short hour that we ate dinner? Do you think it's possible that this suggests a problem with your relationship with being online?

- I noticed that your grades were a little down this semester, and I'm wondering if it has anything to do with your increase in online gaming. Do you feel like you sometimes put gaming in front of doing your homework? What are some ways we can address this concern?

9

Online Identity and Your Digital Footprint

The digital footprint is the documentation of one's identity online. This includes information posted on social media, such as photos and status updates. It also includes information entered into sites for commerce like Amazon or iTunes.

Ever wonder why Amazon can always provide you suggestions about what you might like to buy? It is because they track all of your purchases, as well as all items that you seek or browse on their site, and build a profile of your identity from these behaviors (see Figure 9.1). Most of us are so comfortable with using computers to make purchases, pay bills, and post photos that the digital footprint is not a new phenomenon. For a baby born today, the digital footprint begins on the day of birth when the social security number is logged into governmental computers, and when the happy parents post the first pictures of their newborn on Facebook. However, digital footprints provide some unique risks for today's teens and young adults.

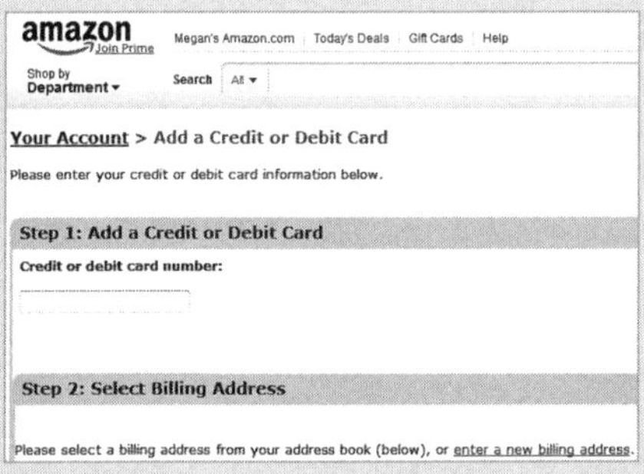

FIGURE 9.1. The popular website Amazon keeps a record of items you purchase or browse.

FIGURE 9.2. These college students are posting about how annoying their professor was in their last class. Will that information embarrass them a few years from now?

The adolescent digital footprint? More like digital vortex.

At least that is how we see many adolescents and even some adults interacting with the Internet. People seem to put anything and everything on the web as though the information will just disappear; a tweet here, a digital picture there, or a check-in on FourSquare that lets others know just where to find you at any given time.

As researchers in this realm and avid social media users, it's hard for us to believe the information that is available on these sites. People will literally post anything, from Twitter tweets of "Ugh, I just threw up in the garbage can #hungover" to Facebook status updates of "Just hooked up with a really cute guy, not sure what his name was ha ha." We've seen pictures showing large amounts of cleavage, friends passed out by the toilet, and the casual passing of a poorly made joint. It truly is incredible the things people, not just adolescents, are willing to put on the World Wide Web. Every day, people are creating and sharing media with their friends, family, significant others, and sometimes even their pets.

Teen Voices   Researcher Voices   Professional Voices   Parental Voices

I am friends with two supposed animals on Facebook, a chimp and a cat.

— Male tween

The type of technology used on social networking sites has created a venue where information can be instantly shared with people in Ecuador, Chile, Italy, Germany, Netherlands, Kenya—you name it.

The Internet offers a 24/7 world of flowing and shared information that can be accessed by a wide audience. It's essential that teens learn how to actively and responsibly participate in this world and in a manner that portrays them in a safe and positive light. Although the debate rages on as to how closely we should guard individuals' online privacy, for the short-term (and probably the long-term), young people remain at risk. Even with privacy policies and laws in place, young people will have important choices about what they choose to share online and the digital "legacy" that they create.

« Where Does Posted Online Information Go?

Much of the information that is collected about us through our online behavior is stored in a data warehouse. A data warehouse is basically a database of information usually used for analyzing and making reports. Many companies and organizations use this data to examine what sites you are using, how long you are on the site, or where you are located. This data is often used for improving a product, or informing advertisements. Because this data is stored, this opens the possibility that other people will access and use that data. As an easy way to

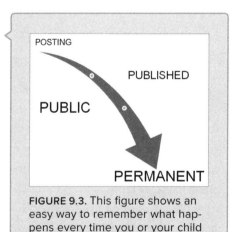

FIGURE 9.3. This figure shows an easy way to remember what happens every time you or your child posts information online.

remind yourself where the information ends up that we post online, you can remember:

POSTING = PUBLIC, PUBLISHED, *and* PERMANENT

It is hard to realize that traces of your identity and personal information are left with each Internet search (your computer's IP address is tracked by many websites) and with each "like" on Facebook. Now that we all have these handheld phones, not visibly connected to anything, we don't see the path our information follows. Therefore it's hard to imagine that it has impact. Once the information is posted, it essentially becomes public property. It becomes published, like this book, and accessible to others. And the information that is posted online is permanently out there, out of your control, and in many cases it can be copied and passed on by others. The reach is nearly infinite.

What Are the Potential Negative » Effects of the Digital Footprint?

The effect of one simple post can be enormous. In 2011 an information technology consultant unknowingly tweeted details of the United States–led operation that killed the terrorist leader Osama bin Laden, as it happened. The tweet "Helicopter hovering above Abbottabad at 1:00 AM (is a rare event)" could have easily blown the cover of the United States and their operation. This is just one of many, many examples that emphasize the power and reach of the Internet and the potential for havoc it promotes. With the click of a button the world can see the things a person posts, if the poster isn't careful. While this example is quite extreme, there are numerous everyday examples that impact teens and their families.

A common situation involving adolescents is the oversharing of personal information, such as posting phone numbers and birth dates on social media sites. This information can be used in several frightening ways, from the rejected suitor who begins to call your teen incessantly, to an identity thief who applies for a credit card using your teen's name and birth date.

Adolescents also frequently provide information about the locations where they can be found—posting their address or the name of their

FIGURE 9.4. Information like a home address is commonly included in statuses or tweets inviting people to events. This information is extremely risky to post. Use a private way of relaying this information such as a message or private event invite.

school on Facebook, or even FourSquare, which provides a real-time map that shows your teen's location.

Another risky piece of information that adolescents frequently post on social media is that they are on vacation. This information can be used by burglars to identify houses to target. You can begin to imagine how this may fit together. An adolescent tweets, "I'm excited to go to Florida over spring break!" on Twitter, and his Facebook profile includes references to his high school by name, and photos of his house and neighborhood. All of this information adds up and provides a potential burglar with the date and location to rob that house.

Beyond providing personal information and location, adolescents may also post information that is inappropriate to share publicly. This information may include risqué or inappropriate photographs, or information about drinking or substance use, or disclosures about romantic relationships or intimacy. These types of displays may put an adolescent at risk for potential emotional, professional, or even physical consequences.

Teen Voices   Researcher Voices   Professional Voices   Parental Voices

Having just applied to medical school last summer, I was extremely cautious as to the information I had displayed on sites such as Facebook and Twitter. Harmless status updates and photos with friends may not send the same impression to a future employer or the Dean of a medical school as it did to your friends.

— Female older adolescent

One current area of controversy involves the Internet, social media sites, and people applying to jobs or professional schools. Employers and admissions committees can and often do access online profiles and search the Internet to find out additional information about their applicants.

Taking risks in portraying an offensive or misleading identity may lead to problems offline. Posting pictures of oneself showing excessive amounts of skin or being overly flirtatious, text referencing any sort of sexual encounter multiple times per week...this may create a damaging reputation for your adolescent's health both mentally and physically.

Teen Voices	**Researcher Voices**	Professional Voices	Parental Voices

A recent study investigated male college students' attitudes toward sexual references on Facebook posted by females. Students viewed and responded to examples of common sexual references including a status update, "Jennifer is sluttin' it up" and a photo of young women in revealing clothing. It became clear that male college students who viewed sexual references on Facebook expected more sexual behaviors from the individual who displays these references. One participant went as far as to say, "If she's willing to put it out on Facebook, why wouldn't she be willing to give it to me?" Further, females who posted sexual references on Facebook were viewed as less attractive dating partners. This study, which we called "sexpectations," suggests that sexual references influence sexual expectations and dating intentions. The study is just one example of how social networking sites have the power to impact reputation and relationships (Moreno 2011).

Legal Aspects of the Digital Footprint »

Most people have some sort of presence online, and this online presence is starting at increasingly younger ages. Because social networking sites are an extension of our personal lives, we are held accountable in both professional and social settings, but also potentially in legal settings. While this may not seem important to a 13-year-old girl posting on her friends' Facebook walls, adolescents should be aware that what they post may hurt them later on. You as a parent need to know what the potential legal aspects of the digital footprint could be so that you can advise and empower your teens to make sound decisions.

Do Adolescents Know about the Possible Legal Ramifications of Posting their Online Information?

In 2012 we conducted focus groups among college students to learn about their knowledge of the legal and professional consequences of Internet use. Despite being tech-savvy college students, the participants were generally unaware of any legal consequences that could occur using social networking sites. However, many students were hyperaware of possible professional consequences in the future. Despite discussing fears and worries about Facebook posts that could potentially impact their chances of getting a job, students were not overly proactive about ensuring privacy on their respective social-media accounts. One of the main reasons that students gave for their lackadaisical attitudes toward privacy is confusion over how to set and maintain privacy on social networking sites. Students who said they had attempted to make their profiles private explained they had little faith that making their accounts "private" even worked or mattered. There was a general feeling of helplessness among the participants; they wanted their profiles to be private but did not know how to ensure their security online.

Legal Issues Parents Should Know About

While in this book we generally focus on concerns related to health, there are a few areas in which we felt that parents would benefit from some understanding of the legal aspects of Internet use. We focused on issues that parents can use to provide valuable support and advice to their teens as they navigate both existing and new Internet sites.

Terms of Service Agreements

The emergence of social networking sites occurred so quickly that it has been difficult to pass legislation as fast as legal issues arise. Therefore, many of our daily actions online are governed by various Terms of Service agreements on each site we use, rather than by a law established by the govern-

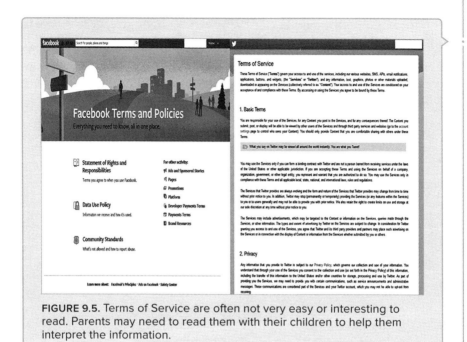

FIGURE 9.5. Terms of Service are often not very easy or interesting to read. Parents may need to read them with their children to help them interpret the information.

ment. Unfortunately, the Terms of Service agreements for many sites are lengthy, with highly detailed information the average reader cannot understand (see Figure 9.5). People must agree or choose not to use the site. More often than not, people will agree to the Terms of Service without thoroughly understanding what the terms are. The students in the focus groups admitted to not reading Terms of Service agreements at all—they simply agreed in order to use the site faster.

College students in our recent research study made various statements regarding their feelings on Terms of Service agreements:

> Every time I read one of those things I don't understand it. And it's long and not worth my time.
>
> — Male college student

> The terms of service have always been something that impedes you from getting to the next step. I'm not going to read it. I just want to go to the next part.
>
> — Female college student

The result is that people essentially give up their privacy and data to SNSs in order to be a part of the online society (whether it is Twitter, Facebook, LinkedIn, Google+ or any others). The new social connections we make are both beneficial and risky. One college student in our focus groups stated: "On Facebook you can literally put your whole life on there, and I think it's harder because you have to trust other people too.... I feel like we put too much trust into Facebook, and it's not actually that private." We need to be aware that our actions online may cause potential harm in the future.

Both parents and adolescents should make themselves aware of the Terms of Service agreements on each social networking site they join. Even though there is little that users can do to change aspects of the agreements, taking the time to read what you are agreeing to will help you and your child understand the risks of using the site.

Legal Case Examples

There have been several key legal cases relating topics discussed in this book, such as privacy and boundaries. Here is a snapshot of three key legal cases to help show how some courts are approaching these issues.

Romano v. Steelcase Inc., 2010
Romano v. Steelcase Inc., 2010 N.Y. Misc. (N.Y. Sup. Ct. Sept. 21, 2010) Social networking sites were a critical source of information in this personal injury case. The plaintiff claimed she suffered permanent injuries, but posted information via Facebook and MySpace revealing she was living an active lifestyle. The defendant sought this information out as evidence. The plaintiff argued her privacy rights would be violated if the information from her personal social networking pages was released, but the Court rejected this argument on the grounds that the plaintiff publicly posted this material on the sites with the purpose of sharing personal information with others.

New York County v. Twitter, Inc., 2012
State of New York v. Harris, (New York 2012), County of New York, 2011NY080152
Twitter was subpoenaed to appear as a witness and present in Malcolm Harris's trial, where Harris was being charged for disorderly conduct in the

Criminal Court of the City of New York. Twitter was to provide "any and all information" regarding Harris's account for a certain period of time. Both Harris and Twitter filed motions to quash this subpoena on the grounds that the subpoena violated the Fourth Amendment, but the judge denied the motions and held "that there is no expectation of privacy when participating in a social media forum like Twitter, so no Fourth Amendment privacy interest would be implicated by the subpoena." Twitter argued that "the order would violate Twitter's terms of service provisions, which state that users retain rights to any content posted on the site, thereby holding a proprietary interest in their content," but the very nature of this social networking site and its ability to share information made the tweets particularly valuable as evidence in determining the status of the defendant.

Dimas-Martinez v. State, 2011

Dimas-Martinez v. State, (Arkansas 2011) 2-11 Ark. 515 No. CR 11-5
Interestingly, citizens who are not committing crimes are also getting themselves into some legal trouble, namely for the improper use of social networking sites while serving on a jury. There are limited statistics on this issue based upon the fact that few cases have been published, but the Federal Judicial Center (FJC) surveyed 952 federal district court judges on jurors' improper use of social networking sites during trial and how the courts were addressing the problem. Thirty judges identified improper social networking site usage, but judges did not have an established process to detect such behavior, suggesting the problem is more widespread due to the lack of an effective detection mechanism.

One notable case regarding social media misconduct on behalf of a juror is Dimas-Martinez v. State. A juror was Tweeting about the case during the trial, and this played a large role in the court's decision to overturn a death penalty conviction. The Supreme Court of Arkansas opinion delivered by Associate Justice Donald Corbin puts the magnitude of social networking sites into context for this case:

> If anything, the risk of such prejudicial communication may be greater when a juror comments on a blog or social media website than when she has a discussion about the case in person, given that the universe of individuals who are able to see and respond to a comment on Facebook or a blog is significantly larger.

The emphasis placed on not tweeting, texting, posting, or doing any-thing electronic was continuously stressed, but the juror ignored this and thus compromised the fairness of the trial. Dimas-Martinez v. State is an illustrative example of how social networking sites can cause legal issues even if you yourself are not the plaintiff or defendant.

The "eDiscovery Law & Tech" blog, which is written by Attorney Patzakis, specifically addresses cyberlaw issues and cases involving social media, and it included an entry in July of 2012 about the number of legal cases involving social media. Part of the blogger's analysis for that entry includes: "The overall tally comes in at 319 cases for this 6-month period, which is about an 85 percent increase in the number of published social media cases over the same period in 2011." However, only a small percent-age of cases have a published decision that is currently accessible online, and Patzakis claims it is likely thousands more exist. Therefore, we should be aware that social media has a more prominent role in legal cases than one might expect, and its impact will continue to increase in the future.

≪ Held Accountable as an Adolescent?

Technology and social media sites will hold individuals accountable no matter what their age. If your child agrees to the Terms of Service, they are held accountable for their behavior. This suggests that the burden of responsibility regarding choices about privacy settings and what to display online falls upon the user. This idea was supported by one of our focus group participants who argued that "the only thing you can really do is self-censor. Don't put stupid stuff up; don't put up anything you don't want other people finding out about, because you're running the risk. Regardless of whether or not you think people are going to identify you or find out your information. If you just avoid talking about anything that could put you at risk, that's the only safe way."

Reinforcing the importance of appropriate self-disclosure via SNSs to your children will help them understand that it is okay to engage and share on these sites but that the sharing has permanent consequences and should be done carefully. Social media sites are useful and beneficial tools, but we must take control of how we use them.

So what implications will SNSs have on our future professional lives? How will technology hold us accountable in the future? College students are becoming more aware of the risks, although there is still much to learn. One male participant pointed out:

> If you don't want it to be a part of your reputation, don't put it out there. Anything you put out there can be used against you. So you have to be careful, and you have to care about what other people are putting up. Not that you even always know.

What Parents Can Do »

Tweens are most likely just getting into the "social media world" and need to be given a lot of direction on what kind of information is okay to share, and what is not. With teens, they may understand that posting something online essentially publishes it to the world but not understand that the information they have shared is globally public and permanent. Given that their thinking is often still in the concrete phase, they may not understand the various groups of people, even in their own lives, who may see the information and use it to make judgments about them.

During middle and high school, many teens are struggling with how to fit in with peers. Sites such as Facebook and Twitter may be venues your child chooses to use in order to make fitting in seem easier. However, the pictures teens might post of a party they attended over the weekend could have major consequences for themselves—and even other participants—if they are involved in sports at school. What may have seemed like a harmless photo depicting a fun social gathering could in turn jeopardize a teen's athletic or academic career.

Older adolescents and college age young adults are probably aware of what posting means, but may make assumptions about how other people will interpret their posts. College students may not take the time to think about their future or how employers or graduate schools will interpret their online identities. College students also tend to generate so much online information that they have trouble keeping track of it or filtering what ends up on the web. There are numerous examples of college-aged young adults who have been denied jobs or entrance into graduate school based

FIGURE 9.6. It's important for teens to be encouraged to think before they post. Parents can remind them about the consequences of inappropriate posts, such as potential employers viewing them.

on content that was displayed on their Facebook profile or Twitter account. As a parent, you should strive to make sure your child is aware of the consequences online posts may have on his or her future career aspirations.

For today's adolescents, one of their many jobs as emerging adults includes managing their online identity and the digital footprint they leave behind every day. Managing your online identity is just as important as managing yourself in a social situation offline.

Parents' Toolkit

1. Tell your teen to treat their online identity like they would their offline identity. Let them know they can stay true to who they are. Encourage them to ask themselves before posting a comment to a question if they would say something like that to a person they just met. Practicing these reminders and little thoughts are the first steps in helping them leave a digital footprint that is positive. These measures will promote balance and integration of your child's online and offline persona.

2. A key message in this chapter is the importance of boundaries. Talk with your teen about what information is and is not ok to post. Make a list together and keep it in a location where it can be referenced later. Some examples of dangerous material to post are illustrated throughout the chapter, and a list is included below:

Do not post online without talking to Mom or Dad

- home address
- phone number
- full birthday, including year
- any information about upcoming or current vacations
- any credit card or bank information

3. Communication about the digital footprint can be incorporated into other strategies discussed in this book. Consider scheduling a social media check-in with your child.

   a. View his or her profile together, and as you do, ask to review the privacy settings.

   b. Discuss the different settings that are available, and if your child has selected strong privacy settings, compliment her on this choice. If settings are too public, discuss changing to a more protective setting and why that is important.

   c. In looking through the rest of the profile, comment on information that is well chosen to be on the page ("That's a great picture of you playing soccer!"), as well as places in which your teen has not joined in with bad behavior posted by others ("I like how you didn't join in on that conversation online about your math teacher.")

   d. These strategies are particularly useful when adolescents are younger so that these check-ins become a normal part of the responsibility of being online.

> ⓘ This chapter's contributors included Megan Pumper, Hope Villiard, Dr. Kerry Gannon, and Lindsay Gordon.

10

Special Health Concerns Connected to the Web: Depression, Fitness, and Eating Disorders

In this chapter we discuss three health concerns that have been shown to have associations with Internet behaviors and exposures.

« Depression on the Web

The Internet, and social media in particular, not only artfully crafts our teens' identities and displays their interests and activities—it also provides a space for the expression of emotions. It is easy to recall the many memories, disappointments, successes, and feelings that overwhelmed us as we endured the transition to adolescence and young adulthood. But what happens when the blank journal page of our youth becomes a computer screen and the pen becomes a keyboard? Simple, the recording of emotions goes digital as well.

In this first section we will address the intersection between emotional health and social media use. We will consider displays of depression on Facebook and the media phenomenon called "Facebook depression."

Why is depression a special concern? Many tweens, teens, and young adults face mental-health problems; in fact, this is the time period is when

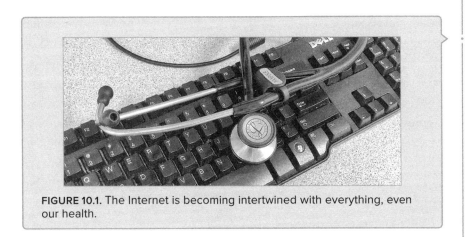

FIGURE 10.1. The Internet is becoming intertwined with everything, even our health.

most mental-health disorders develop. Changes in personal relationships, increasing difficulty of workload, and self-exploration create challenges that can trigger an existing predisposition to a mental illness, and understandably so. The most common mental-health concerns in this population include depression and anxiety. The most common form of depression within the adolescent and young-adult age group is major depressive disorder, which has a yearly incidence of approximately 8 percent (Hunt and Eisenberg 2010). However, an additional 22 percent of adolescents and

FIGURE 10.2. An adolescent may post on social networking sites, such as Twitter, about daily life events that are tied to emotional experiences.

young adults suffer from "subdiagnostic" levels of depressive symptoms, meaning they have symptoms but not the exact pattern of symptoms required to make a formal diagnosis (Yang et al. 2010). Symptoms of depression can include depressed mood, hopelessness, increased guilt, difficulty concentrating, and appetite or sleep difficulties. Both those with a major depression diagnosis and those with depression symptoms experience problems with daily functioning and are at risk for negative consequences (Rohde 2001). Negative consequences of depression include increased rates of substance use, other mental-health problems, and suicide (Rao and Chen 2009).

Identification of mental-health problems depends heavily on adults, especially parents, to recognize that something is wrong. Parents are often essential to getting a teen to a clinic, as many teens rely on parents for resources such as transportation, financial support to be seen by a doctor, and medical consent to be able to receive treatment. Teens often face difficulties in approaching an adult about mental health concerns. Further, many are unaware of their need for help, don't know how to access mental-health services, or simply lack confidence in these services. Presumably, for all of these reasons, the strongest predictor of a child receiving mental-health services is parental recognition of symptoms (Teagle 2002).

How can you as a parent recognize symptoms of depression in your teen? Signs may include becoming withdrawn, showing decreased appetite, or sleep problems. However, many parents argue that these symptoms may be hard to recognize given that many teens exhibit many of these signs as part of normal adolescence! In today's digital world, parents may now find

| Teen Voices | **Researcher Voices** | Professional Voices | Parental Voices |

A previous study by SMAHRT in 2012 illustrated that older adolescent profile owners who displayed depressive symptoms on Facebook were more likely to also score as depressed when a clinical screening tool was used to assess depression symptoms. While we don't suggest that Facebook should be used for depression diagnosis, it may provide clues to which teens are at risk and may benefit from a visit to the doctor's for depression screening (Moreno 2012).

Examples of depression symptoms and how they may be displayed on Facebook or Twitter				
	Depressed mood	Feelings of guilt	Difficulty concentrating	Sleep problems
Facebook	OMG IM SUCH AN EMOTIONAL WRECK RIGHT NOW, I MISS MY FRIENDS SOOOO MUCH UGH :(	broke two things in two days at work...ugh, I'm surprised that I still work there	seriously...staring at the wall when i know that i have homework to do... hello wall	I hate taking a trip then coming back and having to adjust back to real life... so I'll just solve the problem by taking a nap right now
Twitter	all good and great things come to an end	why do I continue to give into things that I know will end #badly	very extremely short attention span in my class right now #lookabird	dying. I need sleep. nowww!

FIGURE 10.3. These are references of potential depression symptoms found on social networking sites. A single post may not mean that depression is present, as many teens use social media to vent emotions. But a pattern of posts could suggest being at risk for depression.

suggestions of depression in their teens through their teens' own Internet use. For example, a teen may express symptoms of depression in their status updates on Facebook or tweets on Twitter. In one of our studies, we found references to either stress or depression were displayed publicly on over 25 percent of young adults' Facebook profiles (Moreno 2011).

Social networking sites can provide another opportunity for adults, including you as a parent, to understand the feelings of tweens, teens, and young adults.

Tiara's story

The details found in 140 characters on Twitter show a powerful interaction between a parent and child:

@TeenzieKat: What a horrible horrible week...I'm amazed at how my life spirals downward.

@DevotedDad: Sounds like someone needs a bubble bath, maybe a hammock, good workout, watch the sunset? It'll get better. #StepByStep

@TeenzietKat: Thank you :)

Although the intended audience may not have included a parent, through utilizing social networking sites the parent was able to gain insight into the emotions and comfortingly intervene without being invasive.

< *What Parents Can Do*

While we all have a bad day now and again and some teens may find it helpful to vent on social networking sites, it is always a good idea to approach your child if you notice repeated postings about negative emotions or feelings on Facebook.

Teen Voices   **Researcher Voices**   Professional Voices   Parental Voices

In a recent study, we asked older adolescents how they would prefer parents to respond if the teen had displayed a reference to stress, anxiety, depression, or suicidal ideation on Facebook. For each of these concerns, students wanted parents to respond with either a phone call or a face-to-face conversation rather than an e-mail or by more subtle means. One adolescent told us, "Be mindful of my mental health and look for the cries for help...and take action via phone or in person."

FIGURE 10.4. Communicating via the computer can give people a sense of security in disclosing their feelings and emotions.

Parents' Toolkit

As feelings are a sensitive topic, many parents may have concerns about how to bring up these conversations. Remember, using an approach that is inquisitive, that is, asking questions, rather than assuming or judging, is helpful to the teen so that he or she feels comfortable opening up. If you begin to notice a pattern that includes repeated posts that meet criteria as a depression symptom, it's time to talk more seriously about how your teen is doing. It may also be time to consider a visit to the pediatrician to help evaluate whether these feelings go beyond the normal "feeling down" of adolescence. If any status updates, comments, or posts suggest suicidal thoughts, they should be taken seriously and require immediate medical attention.

Possible conversation starters include:

"I've been a little worried about how you are feeling lately, I wanted to check in to see if everything is ok with you."

"I noticed a status update you wrote this afternoon about feeling really depressed, I'd like to check in to see how you are doing."

"I have noticed a few times in the last few weeks that you've posted about feeling down on Facebook. I am starting to worry about you a bit, and I'd like to talk with you to see if things are ok." In short, try asking if everything is ok, or asking about what a particular status update meant, rather than assuming that things are terrible.

Facebook Depression: Media Hype, Not Medical Illness

Can Facebook actually cause depression? A 2011 report by the American Academy of Pediatrics raised the question of whether "Facebook depression" exists. They quoted news articles that suggested that spending time on Facebook could lead to higher rates of depression. The media seized on this story, and soon parents began to come into clinic with concerns that their child may catch "Facebook depression" from being online too long. Very little research on this topic exists; one study by our group found no association between time spent on Facebook and reported depression symptoms. While we argue for a healthy balance between online and offline time for many reasons, including promoting good mental health, it appears that warning parents about "Facebook depression" may have been premature.

Teen Voices   **Researcher Voices**   Professional Voices   Parental Voices

A 2012 study examined older adolescents' time spent on Facebook each day for one week using the experience sampling method. Experience sampling method includes sending a series of random text messages to study participants. In this study, the texts asked whether the student was currently online, for how long, and what they were doing online. This method provides a very objective and accurate means to measure Internet use, rather than relying on teens to remember how many times they log on over a day! Older adolescents also took a depression screen as part of the study. The measure of time spent on Facebook was calculated and compared alongside the depression screening results. The results were that there was no association between time spent on Facebook and likelihood of screening positive for depression (Jelenchick 2012).

Finally, while we can be reassuring about Facebook depression overall, it is important to note that for some teens, their experiences on Facebook may lead them to feel more depressed. For other teens it's possible that Facebook can be helpful in lessening their symptoms when they are experiencing depression. Each teen is an individual and will react to various experiences differently. It is worth considering that some teens may struggle with balance in controlling their Internet habits, and this may be a risk factor for negative emotional outcomes. While Chapter 8 tackles Problematic Internet Use, it is worth noting the popularity and frequent use of social media by teens may be a setup for some teens to develop overuse of the Internet.

Overall, in considering the impact of social media on teens' emotional development, it has been suggested by some scholars that Facebook provides a situation in which the "rich get richer," meaning that socially connected and confident teens do well, and the "poor get poorer," meaning that kids at risk may find more opportunities for risk on this site. There are no signs that these sites are going to decline in popularity anytime soon, so more research is needed to understand these questions.

Obesity Prevention and Treatment »
Approaches Through Technology

Obesity is a growing health concern among children and adolescents. Over one third of adolescents between the ages of 12 and 19 are at risk for being overweight and over 10 percent are considered to be obese. Strategies that are targeted specifically to this age group are needed now more than ever to combat this epidemic. Adolescents use a variety of technologies on a daily basis. Could technology help combat obesity or promote fitness?

In this section we'd like to focus on a research study we did that highlights some potential new ideas for the intersection of the Internet and improved fitness. The primary purpose of this study was to investigate adolescents' preferences for technology use related to fitness. We used focus groups with adolescents between the ages of 12 and 18 from urban, rural, and suburban communities across three different states. Topics that were covered in the groups included; definitions of fitness, activities that promote fitness, technology usage, current uses of technology for fitness purposes, school and community resources available for fitness promotion, and future preferences for personal and community technology for fitness improvement.

What we found was that all participants in the groups reported using technology on a daily basis. However, there were differences between younger and older teens in their use of technology to support fitness. Younger participants described technology as a complement to fitness,

FIGURE 10.5. Adolescents using technology, such as the Wii (a video gaming console) and workout videos to stay in shape.

"we're just running and there's nothing to listen to…but when there is music on, everyone feels like 'oh this is fun, let's run around, let's be fun.'" Whereas older participants felt technology was a motivator for fitness: "I mean if I see someone's (Facebook) status is like 'going running,' I'm like wow, I should probably go do that, too, "or, "Whenever you guys say, 'running like ten miles' I'm like…maybe I should."

There were also differences by type of community. Adolescents in rural settings reported consistently using outdoor resources for fitness, "I walk around our property, walk my dog, and just shoot basketball." On the other hand, adolescents living in urban areas more often took advantage of indoor fitness options; "I've got workout videos, like DVDs…and I go to the gym." Adolescents in all communities are exposed to and enjoy video game systems, particularly when they involve physical movement in order to play. For instance one group participant stated, "I got the Xbox Kinect and that's definitely for fitness 'cause everything you do is movin' like your shoulders and stuff…it really gets you moving 'cause you really get into it."

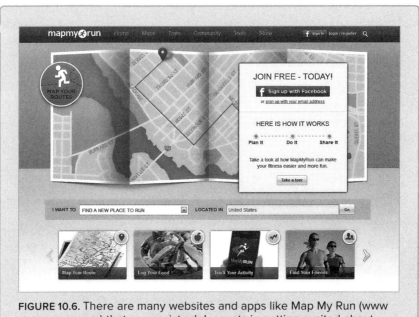

FIGURE 10.6. There are many websites and apps like Map My Run (www .mapmyrun.com) that can assist adolescents in getting excited about exercise.

In summary, adolescents' use of technology does differ by age as well as across communities. Given that the vast majority of adolescents have daily access to technology, which may include iPods, video games, the Internet, and cell phones, there is potential that these technologies can be better directed toward fitness promotion.

What Parents Can Do >

Parents and physical education teachers can encourage their adolescents to use technology for fitness by providing and supporting the use of playful, interactive video games, like those used with the Kinect or Wii video game systems, as part of organized gym or after-school activities. Additionally, they can facilitate joining online social networking sites, like Facebook, which have groups for teens that allow for correspondence about and positive reinforcement of fitness goals. Also, schools and communities can invest in technology such as a GPS linked to a phone or computer that can provide support and encourage teens to meet and set new physical goals. These different options provide ways in which technology can be incorporated to provide accessible and safe resources to accommodate the needs of adolescents across ages and communities.

Body Image and Eating Disorders >>

Adolescents are constantly bombarded with messages about body image in their environment. After age five, risks of eating disturbances increase annually (Stice et al. 1999). These issues can come up from many different types of pressure to be thin, one of which is through media influence.

In current U.S. mainstream media, "beautiful" women are often defined as tall and skinny with little room for any other characteristics. Teens may internalize this thin ideal and model what they think their body should look like using unrealistic images of women in magazines, television, and movies. Men have also been influenced by media images, but commonly in a different way than women. They are pressured to be muscular and "manly," which can similarly cause distress to lose weight and gain muscle mass in order to be what they think society considers attractive (Pope et al. 2000).

FIGURE 10.7. By looking at images like these daily, teens may formulate opinions on their own and other's body images that could potentially have a strong influence.

An unhealthy body image may be related to media exposure (see Figure 10.7); however, studies show that peer and family influence is also critical in the development of poor body image. Peers can create social reinforcement of negative body image through teasing or talking about weight issues of others. Parental modeling has also been an essential part in shaping body image. If a child sees their parents complaining about caloric intake or attempting to monitor their food intake, her or she will grow up with this ideal and could have the same potentially unhealthy habits (Quiles et al. 2012).

Development of Unhealthy Body Image and Eating Disorders in Adolescents

Today about 50 percent of adolescent women and 33 percent of adolescent men are unhappy with their weight; further, about 70 percent of adolescent men are unhappy with the size of their muscles (Mohnke and Warschburger 2011). This dissatisfaction could lead to a distorted body image or attempts to lose weight or gain muscle. In some cases this can lead to changing in eating habits, like diets, binging, vomiting, and counting calories. At the extremes, these changes can lead to eating disorders. Anorexia nervosa is a condition where an individual restricts eating, often through excessive exercising, diet pills, and intense food restriction. Bulimia nervosa is an illness that consists of cycles of binging on food to the point of losing control and compensating through vomiting or laxatives to get rid of the food. Lastly, binge-eating disorder is a more recently studied condition and involves frequently consuming large amounts of food, often done in secret out of embarrassment. These are serious issues: In college-aged students, 2.0 percent had a lifetime prevalence of anorexia, 4.6 percent of bulimia, and 0.6 percent of binge-eating disorder (Favaro et al. 2003).

Can Unhealthy Body Image and Eating Disorders Be Related to the Internet?

We recently conducted a study involving focus groups with female college students. They were asked to discuss the association between body image and Facebook. Additionally, participants addressed their understanding of how age, gender, and advertisements intersect these issues.

Three main themes came up in these groups. The first was that because of the number of people and amount of information accessible on Facebook, the site provides an "ideal medium for [personal] comparison." Female college students described using Facebook to compare themselves to "real" people on Facebook. These real people were more influential and believable for them compared to the "emaciated or muscular models in magazines."

The second theme we found was that females thought there were gender differences regarding how males and females represented themselves through photographs and text. Female college students thought that the traditional gender standards of women focusing on weight and men focusing on muscles were being reinforced. For example, women would post pictures of themselves posing in feminine poses with flattering outfits, men would post pictures of themselves flexing in front of a mirror. The third theme was about peer influence and how a user viewed her own body image. College women noted that if they were to post on Facebook a comment about their body image, they would carefully examine the responses. Similarly, if they posted a photo of themselves that they thought was pretty, they would want to see if anyone else commented that they looked pretty. In summary, they felt that for some people, Facebook is being used as a support system for people to receive reassurance in order to boost self-esteem. Participants thought that if one had a positive body image, they would not feel the necessity to write posts about weight or self-esteem on Facebook.

Through this study we concluded that for females, Facebook is likely to be influential on body image, but it depends on the person's own experiences whether it is a positive or negative influence. If a student is experiencing body image issues, she may portray her feelings about her body online through negative comments about herself. If the person receives positive feedback from peers, the person may feel better. However, if this positive support is not received online (if nobody gave the individual the positive reinforcement they desired) it could hurt the individual further.

Different Types of Body Image Content Online

Social media sites provide a plethora of ways for adolescents of all ages, races, and cultures to express themselves, which could include expressions of body image issues or eating disorders. Facebook enables users to post pictures and statuses, comment on others, and join groups. Some groups are related to promoting eating-disordered behavior. Twitter has users who dedicate themselves to tweeting about weight loss and eating disorders for others to follow. Both of these sites allow users to express any of their feelings, which could be about their body image (see Figure 10.8). Both these sites also allow teens to identify other teens with similar issues, and potentially promote dangerous diets or weight-loss practices.

FIGURE 10.8. Posts like this are seen on social network sites such as Twitter. These types of posts can reinforce negative feelings for the teen who posted it and have the potential to influence the viewer as well.

A final area to be aware of on the Internet, are the sites and blogs that are "pro" eating disorder. The numerous websites promoting eating disorders can often be found by doing an online search for "pro ana" or "pro bulimia." There are even YouTube videos that show people how to vomit with the least amount of mess. Blogging is a similarly popular way to express oneself. Blogs for individuals with anorexia, referred to as "pro-ana," create a way for individuals with anorexia to connect with others to talk about food restriction, how disgusted they are with their bodies, exercising, and how to hide their illness from others (see the example in Figure 10.9). These sites can be dangerous and influential by connecting an at-risk teen with both a community of supporters for unhealthy weight loss or diets as well as with new skills for how to maintain disordered eating.

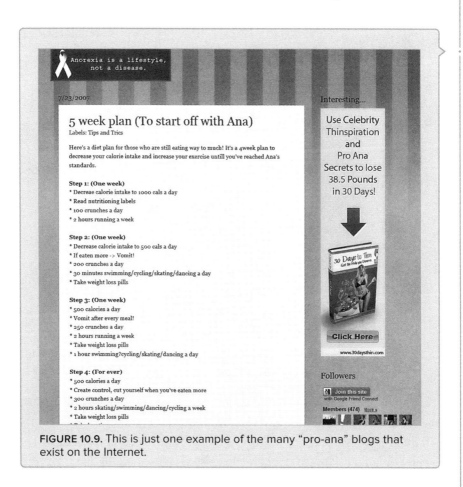

FIGURE 10.9. This is just one example of the many "pro-ana" blogs that exist on the Internet.

< *What Parents Can Do*

There are numerous ways in which parents can talk with their teens about how the Internet can intersect with body image and eating disorders.

Being proactive about body image is the first step to prevent future problems. Talk with your child from the time they are young about what it means to have a healthy weight and the importance of a nutritious diet and enjoyable exercise. Use doctor checkups as a time to reinforce these messages with the help of your pediatrician.

Since modeling is important, being a positive role model is essential—have healthy eating and exercise habits. It is imperative for adolescents to have a positive exercise habits, as they help teens sleep better, feel better, and appreciate the body for what it can do rather than how it looks.

 **Parents' Toolkit**

Ask your child about his body image using language that is direct and non-judgmental. In my clinic we ask all teens during their checkups: "How do you feel about your body image?" You'd be surprised at the insightful and poignant answers we get back!

Talk with your child about what she is seeing online related to weight or body image.

- Ask your child if he has ever looked into diets or weight loss information online. How did he search for it? What kind of information did he find? What information was useful to him?
- Ask your child if she has ever found unhealthy information about weight or fitness on the Internet. How did she come across this information? What did she think about it? Where does this information typically come from?
- Ask your child to show you pictures of people he admires and want to be like, and discuss what a healthy weight or physique looks like.

As your teen gets older and learns about eating disorders in health class, talk with him or her about whether he or she has seen content online related to eating disorders. If so, review the content together and talk about what it means and how it could be dangerous in influencing other teens.

If you think your child is suffering from an eating disorder, discuss the subject in a loving and nonconfrontational way and explain why you are concerned. Schedule an appointment with your pediatrician. The doctor will be able to assess symptoms, provide diagnosis, and screen for medical problems.

 This chapter's contributors included Leah Wachowski, Loren Krueger, and Dr. Erika Mikulec.

11

Ideas for Addressing Internet Safety with Your Teen

Well, now you know some of the risks of Internet use and are well versed on the Healthy Internet Use model of balance, boundaries, and communication applied to specific Internet safety concerns. This chapter ties together some of the big picture themes and ideas for how parents can approach this topic when working with their children at home (or away at school). There may not be one right answer that suits every family. As a parent, you will discover approaches that will work for you and your family. Below are some suggestions that may be useful to consider.

≪ Trust Your Gut Because You Know Your Kid

Not all approaches to Internet safety education will necessarily work for you. However, you know your kids—you've raised them this far and know what they'll listen to, what they won't, and how to get their attention. A lot of what is important to remember about online safety can be taught by transferring how to handle real world dangers (for example, "stranger danger") to those encountered virtually (for example, talking to people you don't know online). You know how to engage your kids in conversation, and you can do a lot for them by simply asking about how they are using the Internet and what they are doing to protect themselves. If your teen wants to join a social networking site, you may choose to set up his account together so you can see what kind of privacy options there are and get a better feel for what the site offers. You may try the site out for yourself. Regardless of your situation and approach, you have the advantage of knowing your kids, and you can help them by providing information they'll listen to and remember.

Collect Available Resources and Choose the Best Ones »

Internet safety is a complicated topic, one that constantly evolves as new websites appear. Fortunately, there are many valuable resources available that can help spark discussion about Internet safety. Numerous doctors' offices, schools, and other community avenues provide handouts at appointments, conferences, or meetings that give a brief overview of Internet safety topics. Additionally, stories seen on TV specials or in newspapers may provide new information. Collect as many of these resources as possible.

They may not all be the perfect tools, but you can choose the best ones for your family. Perhaps you need a great way to start the conversation about safe Internet use with your preteen. A brochure from a doctor's office might be perfect for that age and approach. Even everyday activities can be used to start a conversation about online safety. If your teenager is filling out an application for a summer job, you can use the opportunity to talk about being careful about the digital footprint he or she has created on Facebook that an employer may find.

Know the Sites Your Kids Are Using »

While the risks of Internet use are present on many websites, they may show up in different ways. Each social networking website has a unique set of privacy settings, and each offers a unique way for individuals to express themselves. If your children join a new site, consider not only asking them about how they protect themselves on the site but also experiencing the site for yourself. For example, if you find out your child has created a Twitter

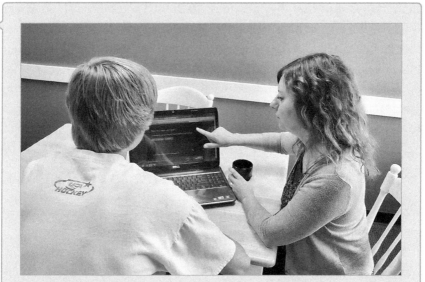

FIGURE 11.1. If you know the sites your kids are using, you can point out areas that might present risks.

account, you might think about starting your own account. You may then have new understanding of the site and be able to offer new information to your son or daughter as well as discuss shared experiences.

≪ Should Parents Get a Facebook Profile?

As a parent, you may choose to use many of the tips and ideas in this book to help your children use the Internet safely, and you may even make a habit of getting to know the sites your children visit. As you think about getting to know these sites, you might give special consideration to Facebook. The website is incredibly popular and continues to be used by almost all adolescents in the United States. You may already be aware of the increasingly complicated features the site has to offer. It therefore may be an especially important site to know a lot about, and to know how your kids are using.

But how do you become and remain knowledgeable about Facebook? One consideration is to create and use your own Facebook account. Given Facebook's enormous popularity, it may bring additional benefits beyond interaction with your child. Some parents use Facebook to plan and promote family events like reunions and others use Facebook to network with other parents and share ideas. On the other hand, some parents feel that Facebook is really just for teens and that adults should not use the site, or that their sons and daughters would view having their parents on Facebook as an invasion of privacy. Parents must make their own choices based on their views and values.

If you decide to join Facebook, you may still wonder how best to use it. Some common questions from parents include:

- Should parents add their children as friends on Facebook?
- Should parents communicate with their children on Facebook?
- If so, how often?
- Should parents chat, message, write on their wall, or do all three?

Teen Voices   Researcher Voices   Professional Voices   Parental Voices

I have spent a lot time on Facebook. Some people update very regularly, sharing thoughts, websites, and other content several times a day, while others may go weeks without ever updating their profiles. A small proportion of people make frequent, sometimes more than daily, references to alcohol and other drugs on their profiles. Some college students have even referred to themselves playfully as "alcoholics," and have later made references to needing to cut back on alcohol use due to poor school performance.

Seeing these posts leads me to wonder about these students' privacy settings. If I can see these posts, who else can? Can friends and family? Can professors from their university? Can prospective employers? And do these students understand their privacy settings well enough to answer these questions, if asked?

Maybe a mother or father who saw these posts would have the same questions as I did, and could use this opportunity to educate her or his child on safe Internet use. Although you may have concerns whether or not you can navigate Facebook or become "friends" with your child, you may find this to be easier than expected.

— Male older adolescent

FIGURE 11.2. Maybe seeing these alcohol-related posts on a Facebook profile would prompt a parent to have a conversation with a son or daughter about drinking patterns, and about the digital footprint.

These questions may lead parents to feel intimidated about how to use Facebook.

However, from our research team's experience, we have come to believe there are positive ways in which parents can use the website.

1. Potential Benefits and Challenges for Parents of Joining Facebook

While many parents have joined Facebook, others may have concern about doing so. In this section we'll help weigh the benefits and challenges of being part of the Facebook community.

Benefits

Just as with any new tool, Facebook presents new opportunities and new challenges to users. It is possible that parents like yourself may experience benefits from having a Facebook account. First, having an account may help you understand the lingo and features of the site. So when your daughter mentions that she "posted a new link" or "updated her Timeline" you will really know what this means. As Facebook is always changing, having an account will help you anticipate and understand these changes, and then be able to advise your teen on what new risks or benefits the changes may bring. Further, if you feel that your teen seems to use Facebook too much, you may be able understand more about the features that teen may be over-using and why. Having your own account may also help you to understand some of the potential risks. You may notice questionable advertisements that pop up and so be able to discuss these with your teen. You may receive weird friend requests and take the opportunity to discuss decisions about friending with your teen from a first-hand perspective.

Should I "Friend" My Teen?

When two Facebook users are "friends" this means their profiles are linked and the content of each profile is accessible to the other user. While having a Facebook account may be advantageous to parents, using that account to friend and communicate with one's children may lead to additional bene-fits. You may find Facebook to be a useful, convenient way to maintain communication with your teens, especially those in college who often live in a different city. For example, the messaging function on Facebook may allow you to send a quick note of support such as, "Good luck on that chemistry midterm!" or ask a brief question such as, "Can you remind me of the dates of your spring break?"

Challenges

Although having an account may be beneficial to a parent, you may have worries that it is not normal or common for a parent to do so. Some parents may also worry about the time it could take to learn and use Facebook, and how to fit this activity into their already-busy days. Further, teens may balk at the idea, or tell parents it is not cool for them to be on Facebook. How-ever, we know that you as a parent of a teen have probably had plenty of other experiences in which your teen told you that you were not "cool." :-)

Having a Facebook account may seem doable to you as a parent, but communicating with your younger teen on the site might seem a bit more challenging. You may think that a child would be unlikely to accept a friend request from you. We have heard stories of some parents who have only allowed younger teens to have a Facebook profile if they accepted their

FIGURE 11.3. To create a Facebook account, you can go to www.face book.com, and start by entering information into the Sign-Up area pictured here.

parents' friend request. Even with a friend link established, some children and young adults may be worried about displaying the same Facebook identity to their parents as they do to their friends. It is important to know that Facebook users can choose what information to display to individual Facebook friends, and that many teens do choose to friend their parents but hide content from them. If you are concerned or curious about this facet of Facebook, ask your teen what they have heard about using the privacy setting to hide content and how they may make use of the setting themselves.

Communicate with Your Children in a Way that Works for You

Although Facebook may be a useful tool for providing support for and maintaining contact with children, it is important for you as a parent to be mindful of the ways in which they do so. Children, as well as parents, may have personal preferences regarding the most convenient, fulfilling, effective method of communication. The quality and quantity of communication may have effects on both parents and children. Thus, it may benefit both parents and children to reflect on their communication, discuss what is appropriate for them, and decide on what works best.

Pay Attention to and Provide Feedback on Your Adolescent's Displays

Whether or not you are friends with your teen on Facebook, it is worth viewing their displayed content. This can happen on a scheduled basis.

Some families schedule weekly check-ins as a young teen starts out using Facebook, and decrease the frequency over time as more trust and experience is developed. Check-ins can also be impromptu; if you walk by your teen who is actively using Facebook, take a moment to ask if you can look at the profile with her. These quick moments can be a great way to promote ongoing monitoring and feedback in a natural way. The following story is from a mother on the subject of worrisome displays:

Mira's Story

Mira, a parent of a college-age daughter, was friends with her daughter on Facebook. After spring break she noticed that her daughter was posting many pictures featuring heavy alcohol use. This prompted her to check in with her daughter to make sure her privacy settings were up-to-date…as she knew that her daughter was soon going to be looking for a job. Mira also took the time to check in with her daughter about alcohol use, to make sure she was staying safe and not driving after drinking. Mira realized that Facebook had provided a key opportunity to offer feedback and guidance in a timely manner.

Although you might doubt the likelihood that a college-age child would change behavior based on a parental lecture, research suggests that parental influence persists into the child's college years. In fact, one study suggests that college students who talked to their parents about any topic, not just alcohol, on a given day are likely to consume less alcohol on that day (Small 2011).

FIGURE 11.4. Although you might not always be able to look over your children's shoulders while they use the Internet, there may be other ways to help keep them safe.

As a final point of support for friending your teen, data collected in one of our ongoing studies suggests that almost three-quarters of freshmen college students' parents have Facebook accounts and are friends with their college student kids. We found that less than a quarter of college students block their parents from seeing content on Facebook. Thus, parents who choose to friend their children on Facebook may find they have access to most of the content on their child's Facebook page.

It is worth noting that out of the students in the research study, only about a third actually communicated with their parents on Facebook at least once per week. This may mean that frequent communication on a social networking site is not right for all parents and teens. Some children and young adults may prefer not to have their parents post on their walls, and parents thus may not know the appropriate way to initiate contact with them on the SNS. Others may find different communication tools like mobile phones to be more personal and more convenient for maintaining contact.

 This chapter's contributors included Bradley Kerr and Meaghan Trainor, MEd.

12

The Role of Communities

We began this book with some foundational information for parents to discuss current trends in Internet use, then provided an ages and stages consideration portion, and also discussed the Healthy Internet Use model, which includes the three-pronged approach of *balance, boundaries,* and *communication*. We then spent the middle part of this book exploring individual topics of Internet safety concerns to identify the current evidence around each of these topics, and apply the Healthy Internet Use model so that parents know how to prevent and intervene with these potential problems. To end this book, we'll provide information for adults who want to go a step farther, to invest a bit more time to learn new ways to promote Internet safety. In this chapter, we'll discuss how parents can work with groups in the community about safe Internet use. We'll bring in several quotes from some of the teachers, school administrators, law enforcement, health-care providers, and parents who participated in our focus-group study concerning their thoughts on new ways for communities to support Internet safety.

Working with Your Child's Peers »

Parents don't need to be told that their children's peers can have a great influence on them. Use this to your advantage when it comes to safe Internet practices. Older teens often know a lot about the Internet and may be able to help teach younger siblings, neighbors, or friends about what sites they should be frequenting and how they should be using these sites. When the advice is coming from someone near your child's age or from a peer who they look up to, staying safe online is more likely to be viewed as the accepted thing to do and even "the cool thing to do" rather than another thing they are being nagged to do by a parent or adult. The advice could come from older youth who you know or through mentoring programs in schools such as Link Crew where seniors help show freshmen the ropes of high school. So round up the neighbor kids and get them talking! As suggested during one of our research studies by a teacher:

> Consider peer educators—where instead of hearing it from an old person who doesn't know anything about Facebook or messaging and is just giving you some line, you hear it from a high-school senior when you're a high-school freshman. I think they're going to be much more receptive hearing it from a peer than from an authority.

≪ Working with Other Parents

As a parent, it can be extremely useful to pull together the resources of those in the community to help everyone learn a little more about Internet safety. Enjoy writing? Start a neighborhood online newsletter or a blog. Know someone at your local paper? Suggest a column featuring online safety tips, useful websites/resources, or lessons learned on the Internet. This could fit in to an existing health or technology column. Involved in the PTA? Talk with other parents and teachers at the meetings to learn about the online situations others have witnessed or experienced. If you lead a youth organization, you might spend a little time at the next meeting or practice to go over safe Internet practices. Even if your role is helping to manage the cheerleading team, you could lead a discussion about online safety. One parent we know led a discussion regarding concerns about posting on Facebook borderline inappropriate pictures from the last football game. If your child has friends over and you see them using the Internet, use it as an opportunity to talk about how to stay safe online and make sure they are using approved websites. The opportunities for Internet education are endless. It just requires a few minutes of everyone's time here and there for adolescents to learn the skills they need to stay safe on the online.

As suggested during one of our research studies by a parent: "I talk to friends, coworkers, a lot. I can tell them, this has happened [to our child online], what do we do? And have you experienced this before? Somebody who has similar children's ages."

The Role of Schools >>

Most teens spend a great majority of their day at school. It is where they learn, interact with peers, and grow as individuals, making it seem like a natural place for online safety education to occur. In many schools, the Internet plays a role in nearly every class. For example, social studies classes may use the Internet to view famous speeches by presidents, while a health class may assign students to look up healthy recipes online. A curriculum for online safety could include a separate class designed to teach adolescents at various stages about the risks, benefits, and safety measures they should be taking in their daily Internet use. Alternatively, each class could include information about the Internet and safety.

What are the barriers to teaching online safety in school? One concern that many teachers have is that kids may know more about the Internet or use different sites from those with which the teachers are familiar. One way to solve this barrier is to teach educators about online safety topics so that they feel more confident in teaching this subject. Teachers, like everyone else, are very busy people and so this education would need to happen at a convenient time. Some potential suggestions include having short lessons at the beginning of staff development days or other staff meetings. These could be great ways to start helping teachers feel more self-assured and knowledgeable about the Internet safety topics. As a result, they will be better able to pass on this understanding to their students and help them stay safe in the virtual world.

How Teachers Can Promote Positive >
Aspects of Internet Use in the Classroom

The school day no longer ends at 3:15. Our students are posting online assignments at all hours of the day and night. They are blogging, video conferencing, file sharing, collaborating, and creating at home, at school, in the car (hopefully not when driving!). Our world is no longer home—school—practice—home. We are connected to all elements at all times.

Educators can use the Internet to instruct and assess students as well as provide them with an opportunity to develop their creativity and analytic thinking. Now students can use blogging, wiki-ing, and podcasting to demonstrate evaluation or creation skills. Edublogs, an education blogging service, offers free blogs for students as well as campus blog clouds to support learning for both students and their teachers by facilitating reflection, questioning, and collaboration. Wikisineducation allows students and teachers to create wikis to share resources and ideas.

The Story of Two Classrooms

Ms. Boerner's Classroom: 3rd Grade English Standard: Identify the speaker or narrator in a selection.

To push her students up the levels on Bloom's taxonomy (educational objectives) as well as increase student engagement, Ms. Boerner incorporates the use of MySpace, which allows the creation of a profile page for an individual or a group, when discussing narrators in text. Students work their way through Bloom's skills together as a class by identifying explicit and implicit information about the narrator. Then with the teacher guiding them, the students eventually synthesize that information and create a classroom MySpace page for the narrator.

Ms. Bennet's Classroom: High School Biology Standard: Describe how human activities and natural phenomena can change the flow and of matter and energy in an ecosystem and how those changes impact other species.

In Ms. Bennet's classroom, students contribute each year to a biological interdependence blog. Students first choose an environmental current-event article to read and reflect on. Past topics have ranged from the Gulf oil spill, deforestation, extinction, and global climate change. After, students write three separate blog entries: 1) an analysis of how human activities or natural phenomena altered their specific ecosystem, 2) what species or biotic factors were affected and how, and 3) propose an action plan to reverse the negative effects of said human activities or natural phenomena. This proj-

FIGURE 12.1. Students working together on a school project, using the Internet in positive ways.

ect incorporates Internet research as well as technological skills to increase student engagement and facilitate learning.

How Can Schools Support Internet Safety at Home?

Schools can be a great avenue to reach families. With families busier than ever, schools could provide innovative ways for parents and kids to learn more about online safety.

Classroom or school newspapers might include blurbs about online safety or provide reliable links that give parents information and kids an interactive website to learn more on the topic.

Workshops could be provided to keep parents up to speed with what the current online trends are and how to protect their kids on the Internet. With all of the other demands on parents' time, incentives such as pizza or free babysitting at the event would help to make attending easier and more enticing.

As suggested during one of our research studies by parents:

I think there is value to having parents and kids together attend a session. So you're both hearing the same information. Because I know, even when I go to something with my child, what I come home with is very different from what my 17- or 18-year-old daughter will think.... I mean really, you know, where, then it's like wait a minute, I'm not sure you're hearing that correctly. I think. And then maybe we can go back and ask, you know, just to be sure.

— Male parent

I think timing for anything is critical. If you can have it on the same night as something else that they're already coming to, you're going to have better attendance. If you have food, you're going to have better attendance. If you, you know, it's just kind of figuring out the right timing of different things, but if you have a captive audience at some point already there, it's best to do it at that same time.

— Female parent

« The Role of Law Enforcement

Law enforcement officials have a unique perspective on the negative effects of poor Internet use from their investigation of crimes such as online identity theft, burglaries (related to online posts about being on vacation), and sexual predation. Many law enforcement groups are already taking steps to create a safe online environment through presentations to kids at school and cyber-safety programs. These groups not only have stories to share about online-related crimes but also can educate both youth and adults on some of the legal ramifications of unsafe Internet practices.

Because of their work in the community, law enforcement are likely to have contacts in local community groups who could be helpful in starting programs about online safety for both kids and adults. These programs can help to bridge the gap between what adolescents and adults know in terms of Internet use.

The following is a list of tips and quotes from law enforcement officials:

1. Be careful with using locations in your Facebook statuses.
"When somebody puts their Facebook status as 'Headed to Puerto Vallarta,' they might as well say, 'Come and rob me.'"

2. Understand that what you put online is permanent and has the potential to be used as evidence in the court of law.
"So there it is, right there on [a teen's] Facebook page, permanent record, literally the evidence that proves he was intoxicated."

3. Beware of online predators—it is easy for a 40-year-old man to pose as a 14-year-old through a computer screen.
"[Kids] would make an [online] Club Penguin date and then they would play, and you do little tasks together and things. So on this site you can actually communicate—you type—and they (the penguins) get the little thought bubbles above their heads, so the penguins seem to talk to each other on the screen. And so, sometimes [this predator] would make a Club Penguin date. He would meet friends online. And there were supposedly safeguards against, you know, pedophiles going on this. But there's not."

"Fake pictures, all this stuff and they're getting these connections with these young girls or young boys or whatever and just grooming them. Grooming them to be exploited."

4. Be proactive with teaching Internet safety.
"Well, they call this generation the digital babies because the minute their feet hit the ground the parents have given them a mobile device, and they're running around and they know how to text. I think the minute they know how to use it, that's when we have to start with the education. Not after something happens…they have their cell phone [then] they have access. Somebody will befriend them, they'll build a relationship, and you know it only takes one time for the kids to get hurt."

5. Online victimization can happen to anyone.
"It's local…it's right here. Sometimes you think that it's kind of like cancer—you think 'I'm never going to get that, not me, it's not going to happen.' That's just not true."

6. Adolescents don't know everything about staying safe on social media like Facebook, even if they frequently use their account.
"We've gotten some of the area colleges involved as far as educating the students as well. But they *think* they've either [already] learned from the schools, otherwise they learn from one another or themselves. I mean we talk and laugh about Facebook and how people are putting all this stuff out, it's because they're self-taught. They don't really know what they're doing. They think 'I have a Facebook account.' Well, you know you got it working, but you really don't know what you're doing."

Health-care providers also have the opportunity to regularly interact with families, making health clinics a great place to teach about online safety. By providing parents with new ideas and reliable resources to explore, parents can feel more confident about what they are teaching their children at home.

Here are some ideas for clinicians to incorporate Internet safety into the clinic setting:

1. During a yearly checkup appointment, online safety could be incorporated into the discussions about limit setting, or in questions about the adolescent's Internet use.

2. In one of our previous studies, we found that even if doctors were not asking patients directly about their Internet habits, parents felt that handouts on the subject given in clinics could help spark conversation about online safety in waiting rooms and at home.

3. Instead of lollipops, clinics could distribute stickers that feature a fun website that teaches kids about Internet safety.

4. For patients who are diagnosed with a minor illness, such as an ear infection or strep throat, give them "homework" to look up information about their illness online with their parents and then discuss it with the patient at the follow-up visit.

The following are some insightful quotes from our focus group made up of health-care providers, including doctors, nurses, and medical assistants:

I think that any opportunity that's brought up to you—if it's a pamphlet from the school or the doctor's office—that's when we can reiterate again the importance of [online] safety.

— Nurse

FIGURE 12.2. Pamphlets can be a way to spread the word about Internet safety.

There might be a role for our medical assistants in terms of talking to patients [about online safety]. That would be the closest we would get to a peer that would be naturally involved in a visit.

— Medical assistant

Yeah, information in pediatrician and family practice offices where kids are seen for their health problems or routine physicals or pre-school physicals, things like that, that would be a place to maybe bring it up with younger people.

— Nurse

Community Groups »

Many of the parents and community members we talked to emphasized that teaching online safety is not a job that should fall solely to teachers, parents, or any individual group—it should be a multisystem approach, coming from many different directions. In other words, educating youth and adults about Internet safety needs to be a community effort. Here are some particular groups who may be helpful in supporting online safety education:

- Local news: Ask your local news station to provide an Internet safety series.
- Libraries: Some libraries provide Internet safety classes. For teens to be provided a computer access code to use at the library during future visits they must complete an Internet responsibility class. Other programs promote safe Internet use focused on reading or community engagement.

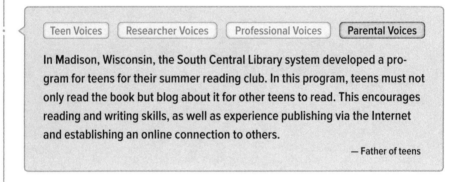

In Madison, Wisconsin, the South Central Library system developed a program for teens for their summer reading club. In this program, teens must not only read the book but blog about it for other teens to read. This encourages reading and writing skills, as well as experience publishing via the Internet and establishing an online connection to others.

— Father of teens

≪ Churches

Some churches include Internet safety as part of family activities. One church we knew had a "grandparents" night to teach them about social media trends and how to help protect their grandkids! Churches can incorporate an Internet safety night for teens or teach Internet safety during a family night. One approach might be to have the teen be the tech "expert" and teach the parent an Internet skill, such as how to set up a Facebook profile. Then the parent gets to teach the teen a safety skill. One parent described her church's approach to us:

Almost every Sunday our pastor talks about Facebook and the consequences [of] what you put out there is out there for everyone to read, sometimes a permanent thing that you can't get rid of. [At the church] we're stepping in as a community, wherever your community is stepping in, you know, I think it's kind of everyone's responsibility to, you know, help out in that area.

All Together Now... »

The community can get involved in countless ways—whether it is printing online safety tips on grocery bags or creating short vignettes to read while you wait at the DMV—online safety can be conveniently incorporated into the places people go to frequently. There is a role for everyone. If everyone spends just a few minutes discussing Internet safety and finds a way to incorporate it into what they are already doing, kids will hear several methods they can use to stay safe online from a variety of perspectives, creating a well-rounded Internet safety education. Take a look at the activities you are involved in and see if there is a place where you can help share what you now know about staying safe online.

 This chapter's contributors included Sara Klunk.

13

What's on the Horizon? Insights from the Front Lines of Internet Safety

For this final chapter we wanted to leave you with a sense of optimism. We interviewed professionals and community members around the nation who are on the front lines of Internet safety education: health-care providers, teachers, social workers, and researchers. We asked for their comments on the most pressing issues they face on the topic, the resources and programs they currently use, and what ideas they have for the future. Here are their thoughts.

» Perspectives on the Most Pressing Internet Safety Issues of Today

While big national studies such as the Pew Internet and American Life Project can give you as a parent a sense of what is going on statistically at the national level, it can be helpful to hear from people who are interacting with teens every day. Dr. Lindsay Thompson, a pediatrician with experience and interest in safe Internet use, provides some thoughts on the big picture of how we can consider the important issues that face our teens:

> Since the Internet is here to stay, we, as pediatricians—and parents ourselves—need to figure out how to help adolescents differentiate

for themselves what is true, reliable, or trustworthy, and not just ignore its important social function by advising that children stay away from it. This has to be done with mentoring through adults' use of the Internet.

Often it is our schoolteachers who see and experience teens' day-to-day interactions with the Internet, and teachers often have a solid sense of what risks are common. Randy Cash is a middle-school teacher in New York. He often incorporates technology into the lessons he gives his early adolescent students every day. As such, he is also exposed to teens' risky behaviors and the negative consequences from their Internet use, such as what he describes here:

> I believe that pictures can come back and haunt them (Internet users) years after they are posted on social networking sites. The fact that most [teens] don't ever check their privacy settings, those images can end up anywhere. With younger students, they tend to give out more private and personal information without any thought of where it may go. Most students don't know, and their parents are even further in the dark about what is happening.

A similar perspective is offered by Elizabeth Goodspeed, a high-school teacher in Illinois. She serves as a student advisor to teens during the college application process and finds that many teens who apply to college are surprised to learn that their online behaviors—both academic and social—become part of the college admissions process. She states:

> From my experiences in the high-school setting, I'd say that helping students truly understand their "digital footprint" and helping them become more savvy and literate as participants in the world of social networking and online photo sharing sites should be key areas of focus in working with teens on Internet safety.

Another set of concerns about the Internet is raised by Josie Boromisza, a high-school teacher in a rural community. While many of us grew up with the idea that smaller communities were often safer for kids, the Internet provides a way for global risks and benefits to enter these communities. Mrs. Boromisza describes some of the risks she has seen her students face:

There are many pressing Internet safety issues for teens today. Probably one of the most threatening is one of online predators. I realize that the Internet grants access to all kinds of morally questionable material, but I believe the biggest threat for teens is when predators pose as "friends" while actually being sexual or violent offenders. There are some teens that justify the safety of this type of communication based on a picture. They feel a false sense of security when they can see the person they are in contact with when in reality they can be looking at a picture of anyone.

Mrs. Boromisza also commented on the impact of the many technological devices that students use and their impact on students' abilities to learn and interact with others at school. She states:

With the many portable devices available today, related distractions often [occur while] … behind the wheel. Now more than ever teenagers feel the need to be constantly connected, whether that is while driving or sitting in a classroom. Even if these devices are not allowed in schools they still provide another distraction for students. Many of today's teens are continuously thinking about too many things at one time. It is a form of multitasking but without being fully attentive and efficient in any one task.

FIGURE 13.1. A tween checks her e-mail while walking to school

This concern for overuse of the Internet is echoed by Dr. Wendy Sue Swanson, a pediatrician and blogger at Seattle Children's Hospital. She writes:

I think the most dangerous things teens do is become fairly addicted to their phones. They sleep with them, they eat with them, they drive with them. They sometimes continue to text while "talking" to me in the office! They're changing the way they interact with the natural world…and this potentially (without clear understanding of the consequences) may be the biggest threat as they age.

A final thought to tie these concerns together comes from Dr. Scott Harpin, a public-health nurse and researcher from Minnesota. Working in both academics and community, he provides a way to consider concerns he has seen from both these perspectives:

> There are two areas I think are most pressing in terms of safety. The first lays in how new users, sometimes across the lifespan, experience any technology new to them. This is often more important for early-aged adolescents who have trouble discerning safe "friends" to connect with. Kids who get the chance to sign-on to a cool site for the first time may be blinded at this new experience and more vulnerable to safety issues then.
>
> Related to this is how adolescents in other countries experience the technology without the safety mores that we've experienced over time in the United States. For example, [sex] trafficking in other countries may be facilitated by social networking sites, the adolescents are all the more valuable since the emerging technologies are so incredibly new to those societies.
>
> The second in my mind would be the lip-service given to the importance of Internet safety, with little or no follow-through from parent, school, or advocacy groups on actually implementing safety education programs. Like a clinician who has a myriad of health prevention messages to offer a young person during a clinic visit, I'm guessing there are many efforts that parent groups invest time in, and Internet safety may be left off the list of important issues to cover.

These concerns are no doubt familiar to you after reading this book, and echo how these Internet concerns are considered important across different professional groups and varying communities. Your family or community may be more worried about some of these issues than others, but having the perspective to understand the range of current issues can help you as a parent to educate your child and prevent negative consequences.

≪ Internet Safety Issues Differ by Age: Middle School, High School, and College

As a pediatrician, Dr. Lindsay Thompson cares for children from birth through the end of college. As such, she has discussed Internet safety with parents of children of all ages and how to understand parenting strategies regarding Internet use at these different ages. She describes how these age differences may impact her advice to parents:

> Younger children are more vulnerable to predatory behaviors, so I would limit their interaction with social media. However, as they get older, they should be allowed more affordances, hopefully having obtained judgment of when to ask parents or other adults for help with online interactions, even with the health-care system.

Similarly, Dr. Hanita Oh-Tan also sees children of all age groups in her pediatric practice in Virginia. She raises the important point that children's ability to think about their own safety behaviors varies across ages. She considers this important point when counseling her patients:

> Their mental and emotional understanding of personal safety (even outside of the Internet) differs in these age groups. Being a minor and underage obviously makes many things more severe, possibly with legal implications. Preteens/young teens tend to have more impulsivity—they may act upon something because they think it's "cool" or socially acceptable at the time, but do not realize the consequences.
>
> College students may have a little more understanding and control, but at the same time may feel invincible—and therefore make mistakes, thinking "Oh it would never happen to me." Older teens/college kids may also be more likely to have finances to get into other trouble—making unsafe or illegal purchases. They also may be more likely to be under the influence of alcohol or drugs, [which leads] to poor judgment.

Some people we talked to about this topic focused on contrasts between middle school and high school, common ages in which adolescents begin to use social media and have more independence in their Internet use. Dr. Wendy Sue Swanson considers differences between the needs of middle-school students and high-school students regarding parental supervision as follows:

> I think middle schoolers need a bit more supervision. By the time high school comes, parents have receded and aren't following along, so teens lack any great feedback or leadership or partnership at times to understand the implications of their sharing online.

Dr. Scott Harpin also emphasizes the importance of supervision during the middle-school years because of the emerging role of social media during those years. He states:

> Many young people are socialized into social media during, or even by, their middle-school years. So my guess is they are far more vulnerable to "predatory" types of behavior when they are first signing in to new sites and building their cadre of "friends" or contacts. Certainly, in the high-school years, I think adolescents are a bit more savvy in watching for creepy people outside of their circle. But the potential for Internet bullying is a far bigger issue for these groups of younger and middle adolescents, particularly when hurtful language can be posted with little detection by adults.

FIGURE 13.2. An adolescent studies at a coffee shop while chatting with friends via Facebook IM.

Teacher Elizabeth Goodspeed focuses on providing education about Internet safety as discussions and reminders, rather than as lessons and involving supervision. She writes:

As a high-school teacher, I feel kids need to be reminded/taught how their online activity can have an impact in school settings (and eventually job settings). Discussions about subjects such as: online bullying, posting of online pictures (especially provocative shots and those including displays of illegal activities), and limiting the amount of personal information/behaviors that's shared online seem to be most pertinent to the high-school and college-age students.

« Tell Us about a Potential Future Program or Research Ideas to Improve Internet Safety

When we asked parents and professionals to give us insights about potential programs on Internet safety, we learned about amazing possibilities that could be created in schools, community groups, and clinics. As you read through these ideas, consider how they could be implemented in your own community or home. Talk to your school about whether this type of research program or teaching curriculum may fit in to existing programs. Talk with your clinic about whether they partner with any pediatric research groups, such as the Pediatric Research in Office Settings (PROS) group of pediatricians that has conducted some studies on Internet safety. Dr. Hanita Oh-Tan describes the need for more understanding of Internet safety among children through additional research. She writes:

> I'd like to see more surveying children of various age groups: What have they learned about Internet safety? What are the risks? What kind of information is okay to share? What kind of information is not? What would you do if…? Who taught you these things?
>
> Program ideas could include classes through school to teach about these topics, as well as classes for parents! School-/police-organized discussions [entitled] "How to think critically about what you find online" would be helpful, and they could include sample or fake websites to discuss.

Others whom we talked with described how future programs should target vulnerable groups, such as homeless street youth. Some people may underestimate these communities' access to the Internet. There are many stories about homeless teens using the public library to access the Internet and learn about the location of a food bank or shelter. Dr. Harpin writes:

> I think that even the most vulnerable homeless street youth have access to Internet technologies, and even report having smart phones. These sites and telecommunication modes might be an important best bet for gaining access to these vulnerable youth and getting them prevention messages in ways not available to us before.

Other researchers described use of the Internet or smart phones for reducing injuries, such as through drunk driving. Given the widespread use of the Internet among adolescents, these tools may have broad reach in this population. Dr. Jennifer Whitehill from the University of Washington writes:

> I'm a public health researcher interested in harnessing mobile Internet and social network technologies to prevent injuries, which are the leading cause of death for young people. I'm currently working on a project to understand how Twitter can be used as a tool to prevent alcohol-impaired driving. We are trying to identify older adolescents and young adults whose tweets indicate a risk of drinking and driving and develop ways to respond to them with resources to facilitate safe transportation. If effective, these tools could help reduce the ongoing problem of drinking and driving.

Dr. Heather Royer, a nurse practitioner and researcher at the University of Wisconsin-Milwaukee, is interested in using technology to provide sexual-health information via the Internet so that older adolescents can get information that is accurate and answers to their most important questions. She also has an interest in educating young women about the role of sexual reference displays on intimate relationships as well as in examining the role of social networking sites in identity development among adolescents.

For many of these ideas, it is possible to consider engaging with other teens to promote the program. As we've discussed previously, older teens are fantastic role models for younger peers, and are likely to be persuasive role models. Dr. Scott Harpin writes:

I think some sort of peer monitoring program may be an important future research idea to consider. There could be safety education done passively with "seeds" or influential kids in a high-school or social-network setting who do their best to watch for Internet bullying, sending pro-social messages to stop verbal abuse and/or report to adult mediators of the behavior.

≪ What Work Are You Currently Doing that Involves the Internet as a Positive Contributor to Health or Education?

We were amazed at the diverse and creative programs that exist to engage adolescents of all ages in positive Internet use. Not surprisingly, several examples came from school-based programs. We have followed John Chase's work in his middle-school classroom for several years and are continually amazed at how he integrates positive Internet use into so many different types of lessons. Many of his lessons involve having students take the products of their learning and use them to educate others. John Chase states:

> In my classes I focus primarily on promoting digital citizenship and positive interactions using the Internet and social media. Rather than post a video of your friends bullying a student, why not create and upload a video to YouTube that encourages people to volunteer or adopt a pet from an animal shelter? Not only is this a proactive way to promote civility, but over time you begin to break down the bystander mentality of so many young people, and they begin to realize that they have the ability to make a positive difference in the world, rather than add to the negativity.

Two high school teachers, Luanne Bigbear and Josie Boromisza described an assignment in which students use the Internet to explore connections within a project:

> We have students conduct a research project in which students choose a "monster," which is an illness, a crime, or a natural disaster that plagues society (and ideally something that the student feels a connection with). Then the students conduct research on the issue

as well as the research on the "hero" (or heroes) that are in place to assist a person or people coping with or conquering the monster. Students then create a paper and/or presentation around their monster/hero inquiry. This Internet-based research project has had a powerful impact on the community in my classroom. We believe the students find the project engaging, interesting, and cathartic, and it shows a genuine connection between themes in literature and real life, which is so important for engaging teenagers in any content area.

Dr. Royer explains how the Internet can be used to improve health care for challenging conditions, such as sexually transmitted infections. In Chapter 5 we discussed how many adolescents already use the Internet to investigate answers to their sexual-health questions. Placing reliable health information online is a key strategy to reach out to adolescents and answer their questions. Dr. Royer writes:

> I have developed a web-based intervention to improve the self-management of sexually transmitted infections among young women. Right now I am researching the role of online social networking to

FIGURE 13.3. A group of adolescents sit together at lunch but communicate with their phones rather than talking with each other.

facilitate social support for these patients, which is foundational to improving the self-management of sexually transmitted infections.

Dr. Meg Lederer, a pediatrician in Colorado, was curious about how older adolescents learn Internet safety skills. She set up a project to talk with college students about this topic. She writes:

> During my pediatric residency I worked with a colleague to discuss Facebook privacy with college women in a series of focus groups. Our work was not only fun to complete but also opened our eyes to where these women get information about Internet safety (mostly from each other!) and what motivates them to make changes to their privacy settings. It really highlighted how little information is out there for college students about Internet safety and privacy.

Dr. Allison Pollock, a pediatrician from Wisconsin, saw that adolescents with diabetes were often using the Internet to communicate with friends, but there were few resources for them to learn about diabetes online. She writes:

> I'm currently working on a research project looking at how online resources can best serve children with type-1 diabetes. The project involves a survey asking children how they use online resources, including websites, mobile apps, social networking, and other tools, to understand and manage their diabetes. In addition to learning about what online resources they use, the study explores what types of questions and concerns would still trigger a call to the medical provider. The ultimate goal of this project is to help patients with diabetes choose rich, practical, and safe online resources that will bolster a healthy transition into independent diabetes management in adulthood.

Dr. Oh-Tan, a pediatrician in Virginia, describes a project that her community worked together to bring about. This shows how a group can work together to bring valuable resources to their community. She writes:

> We implemented i-SAFE Inc. into our county schools: http://www .isafe.org/fcps. A little bit about the site: "i-SAFE Inc. is the leader in

e-Safety education. Available in all 50 states, Washington, D.C., and Department of Defense schools located around the world, i-SAFE is a nonprofit foundation whose mission is to educate and empower youth to make their Internet experiences safe and responsible. The goal is to educate students on how to avoid dangerous, inappropriate, or unlawful online behavior. i-SAFE accomplishes this through dynamic K–12 curriculum and community outreach programs to parents, law enforcement, and community leaders. It is the only e-Safety foundation to combine these elements.

It is our hope that this chapter will provide you with a broader perspective. Many other professionals share concerns about how our adolescents interact with the Internet, and many have taken steps to create projects and programs toward improving Internet safety education. We wanted to end this section with these ideas and hopes so that you too are inspired to help promote safe Internet use in your home and community.

‹‹ About the People We Interviewed ››

Luanne Bigbear holds a Masters in Teaching from The Evergreen State College in Olympia, Washington. Her endorsements include English, social sciences, and art. She currently teaches at Shelton High School in Shelton, Washington, and has been teaching since 2006.

Josie Boromisza has worked as a high-school teacher since 1996 with teaching experience in both Washington State and New York State. She specializes in teaching English/language arts and social sciences. She holds degrees from The Evergreen State College and Saint Martin's University in Washington State.

Randy Cash currently teaches 6th through 8th grade media literacy. He has been a middle-school teacher for over 20 years teaching history, social studies, geography, and technology.

John Chase has been a 7th through 12th grade social studies teacher for 24 years. During that time he developed an art and media integration curriculum and program that helps young citizens to develop critical skills, essential for participation in a modern democratic society. He is also the founder and director of M.U.S.I.C., a nonprofit 501(c)(3) publicly supported organization that promotes the educational use of songs by teachers in all subject areas.

Elizabeth Plank Goodspeed has been a social studies teacher, track and field coach, and adviser (academic and social counselor to a group of 25 high-school girls as they move through their years at NTHS) for 17 years at New Trier High School in Winnetka, Illinois. Over the years, she has been a member of several faculty committees that have worked on digital literacy and awareness projects for students.

Scott Harpin, PhD, is an Assistant Professor at the University of Colorado College of Nursing. He has spent 15 years as a public health nurse, working mostly

186

with children in out-of-home placements (foster care, homeless, residential treatment, and juvenile delinquent).

Meg Lederer, MD, is a recent residency graduate working in Denver, Colorado, at two pediatric emergency departments. She writes, "I have always cared deeply about and enjoyed my adolescent patients the most and plan to have a teen focus in my future work in pediatrics."

Allison Pollock, MD, is currently a pediatric resident at the University of Wisconsin, at the American Family Children's Hospital in Madison, Wisconsin. Dr. Pollock completed her undergraduate education at the University of Wisconsin–Madison, with a bachelor of science in mathematics and history. She graduated medical school from the University of Rochester School of Medicine and Dentistry. Following completion of a pediatrics residency, Dr. Pollock will enter fellowship training in pediatric endocrinology.

Hanita Oh-Tan, MD, is a general pediatrician in private group practice in suburban Washington, DC. She is a mother to two children, ages four and six.

Heather Royer, PhD, FNP-BC, is an Assistant Professor at the University of Wisconsin–Milwaukee. Her program of research aims to examine innovative technologies to improve sexual health among adolescents and young adults.

Wendy Sue Swanson, MD, is a general pediatrician and author working at the intersection of medicine and media in hopes of revolutionizing how parents and children access health information and strengthening tools for them to build improved relationships with their doctors and each other.

Lindsay Thompson, MD, MS, is an assistant professor of Pediatrics and Health Outcomes and Policy. Her areas of interest and expertise include pediatric health outcomes in primary care and medical professionalism in social media.

Jen Whitehill, PhD, is a postdoctoral fellow at the Harborview Injury Prevention & Research Center in Seattle, Washington. She is a public health researcher interested in harnessing mobile Internet and social network technologies to prevent injuries, which are the leading cause of death in young people.

« Contributor Bios »

The following people contributed to chapters in this book; most are current or alumni members of the Social Media and Adolescent Health Research Team (SMAHRT).

Kaitlyn Bare worked with SMAHRT between 2009 and 2012. Her area of interest has been how adults can teach Internet safety in clinic, community, and school settings.

Libby Brockman is currently a research assistant and graduate student in public health. She joined SMAHRT in 2008. Her projects have included evaluation of disclosures of health risk behaviors on social media profiles, as well as ways in which adolescents are willing to interact with adults using social media.

Jon D'Angelo, MS, is currently a PhD student at the University of Wisconsin Communication Studies program. He joined SMAHRT in 2012, and his research projects have included evaluation of communication about substance use on social media and its impact on intention to use substances. He is interested in ways in which health professionals and patients could communicate using innovative technologies.

Kerry Gannon-Loew, MD, is a pediatric resident at the University of Wisconsin–Madison. She graduated from the University of Wisconsin Madison School of Medicine and Public Health in 2012 and worked with SMAHRT between 2009 and 2012. Her research interests include how adolescents represent both risk behaviors and protective behaviors on social media.

Natalie Goniu is currently an undergraduate student at the University of Wisconsin–Madison majoring in neurobiology. She joined SMAHRT in January of 2011. Natalie has worked on several research projects, including an evaluation of alcohol and substance displays on Facebook, and the influences of parents and the media on adolescent nutritional habits.

Lindsay Gordon is currently an undergraduate student at the University of Wisconsin–Madison majoring in Journalism and Mass Communication. She joined SMAHRT in May 2011. Lindsay's research focuses on the legal aspects and ramifications of older adolescents' social media disclosures.

Allison Grant, MS, is currently a graduate student at the Colorado State University. She worked with SMAHRT between 2009 and 2011. Allison's research includes an assessment of how friends online and offline influence alcohol consumption.

Lauren Kacvinsky is currently a research specialist. She graduated from the University of Wisconsin–Madison in spring of 2012. Lauren has been with SMAHRT since 2010. Lauren's research interests include ways in which peer leaders on college campuses can use Facebook to identify at-risk students.

Loren Krueger is currently a medical student at the University of Wisconsin School of Medicine and Public Health. She joined SMAHRT in 2012 through the Shapiro Summer Research Program. Loren's current research explores the motivations behind Facebook displays of mental-health disorders and desired interventions to these displays from peers, parents, and health-care workers. Loren's future goals include expanding her work to create social media suicide interventions.

Bradley Kerr is currently a research coordinator. Brad graduated from University of Wisconsin–Madison in 2010 with degrees in Psychology and English and is currently in a Master's in Higher Education Administration program. He joined SMAHRT in July of 2011. Brad has contributed to several projects, including evaluating Facebook profiles and exploring ways in which college students can use social media to communicate with their parents.

Rosalind Koff is a currently a graduate student at Georgetown University in the Communication, Culture & Technology Master's Program. She worked on SMAHRT between 2010 and 2011. Roz worked on several research projects, including college student evaluations of alcohol marketing messages and student perceptions of personal technology use. Roz is currently involved in a project involving a content analysis of user-generated media depicting substance use on YouTube.

Rajitha Kota, MPH, is currently a research assistant on SMAHRT. Rajitha received her Master of Public Health degree in 2012 from the University of Wisconsin–Madison. She joined SMAHRT in September of 2011. Her current research involves studying cyberbullying among college students. She is pursuing a career in medicine and is especially interested in preventative medicine and global health.

Sara Klunk is currently an undergraduate student at the University of Wisconsin majoring in Business. She joined SMAHRT in 2011. Sara's research interests include ways in which parents seek information about online safety, including an assessment of currently available web resources.

Erika Mikulec, MD, is an Obstetrics and Gynecology resident at the University of Wisconsin–Madison. She graduated from the University of Wisconsin School of Medicine and Public Health in 2012 and worked on SMAHRT between 2009 and 2012. Dr. Mikulec's research interests include how social media use impacts adolescents' fitness, and how it could be used to motivate fitness efforts.

Megan Pumper is currently a research specialist with SMAHRT. She graduated from the University of Wisconsin–Madison in 2012. Megan joined SMAHRT in 2009. Megan's research interests include ways in which social media use impacts the mental health of adolescents.

Sarah Rastogi, MD, is a pediatrician and college health physician at the University of Wisconsin University Health Services. She worked on SMAHRT between 2009 and 2011. Dr. Rastogi worked on several research projects, including college student's attitudes toward privacy settings on Facebook.

Shannon Rojecki is a preschool teacher and mom to Cassidy, Carter, and Lucy. Shannon contributed content as well as photographs to this book. Shannon's daughter Cassidy also contributed content.

Shari Schoohs is currently an undergraduate student at the University of Wisconsin–Madison, majoring in Psychology with a certificate in Business. She joined SMAHRT in January of 2012. Her research interests including cyberbullying as well as how alcohol messaging influences college students. Shari intends to pursue a career in higher-education counseling.

Kim Schuchardt is an administrative assistant and parent, and her children Marissa, Drew, and Claire contributed content and reviewed chapters. They also contributed to the photographs.

Ellen Selkie, MD, is an Adolescent Medicine fellow at Seattle Children's Hospital. She worked on SMAHRT between 2008 and 2009, doing a research study involving focus groups with teens about using technology to access sexual-health information. She currently cares for adolescents in the Seattle area and is developing further research on the ways teens can interact with technology to stay healthy.

Mara Stewart is currently an undergraduate student at the University of Wisconsin majoring in Gender and Women's Studies. She joined SMAHRT in 2011. Mara's research interests include how social media use influences tobacco and drug use among older adolescents.

Meaghan Trainor, MEd, is currently a medical student at the University of Wisconsin School of Medicine and Public Health. She joined SMAHRT in May 2012. Meaghan's past work included teaching for the Teach for America program. Meaghan's research interests include evaluating college student alcohol and drug use through Facebook, particularly focused on evaluating what experiences early in adolescence create risky drinking behavior in college.

Hope Villiard is currently a medical student at the University of Wisconsin–Madison as part of the Wisconsin Academy of Rural Medicine. She worked on SMAHRT between 2009 and 2012. Her research projects included an assessment of how fitness is represented on Facebook.

≪ References ≫

Chapter 1

Chen, S. Y., and Y. C. Fu. 2009. Internet use and academic achievement: Gender differences in early adolescence. *Adolescence* 44: 797–812.

Childs, M. 2010. Facebook surpasses Google in weekly US hits for first time. *Businessweek*. http://www.businessweek.com/news/2010-03-17/facebook -surpasses-google-in-weekly-u-s-hits-for-first-time.html (accessed July 1, 2012).

Christakis, D. A., and M. A. Moreno. 2009. Trapped in the net: Will Internet addiction become a 21st-century epidemic? *Archives of Pediatrics and Adolescent Medicine* 163(10): 959–60.

Ellison, N. B., C. Steinfield, C. Lampe. 2007. The benefits of Facebook "friends": Social capital and college students' use of online social network sites. *Journal of Computer-Mediated Communication* 12:1143–68.

Rice, E. 2010. The positive role of social networks and social networking technology in the condom-using behaviors of homeless young people. *Public Health Research* 125:588–95.

Chapter 2

Casey, B. J., S. Getz, and A. Galvan. 2008. The adolescent brain. *Developmental Review* 28(1): 62–77.

Cox Communications and the National Center for Missing and Exploited Children. 2012. New challenges in the battle to keep kids safe online. http:// www.multivu.com/mnr/56493-cox-national-center-for-missing-exploited -children-keep-kids-safer-online (accessed June 1, 2013).

Survey on Facebook user demographics. *Consumer Reports*. http://pressroom .consumerreports.org/pressroom/2011/05/cr-survey-75-million-facebook -users-are-under-the-age-of-13-violating-the-sites-terms-.html (accessed March 14, 2013).

Chapter 3

Lenhart, A., M. Madden, A. Smith, K. Purcell, K. Zickuhr, and L. Rainie. 2011. Teens, kindness and cruelty on social network sites. http://www.pewinternet.org/Reports/2011/Teens-and-social-media.aspx (accessed March 14, 2013).

Patock-Peckham, J. A., and A. A. Morgan-Lopez. 2006. College drinking behaviors: Meditational links between parenting styles, impulse control, and alcohol-related outcomes. *Psychology of Addictive Behaviors* 20:117–25.

Walls, T. A., A. M. Fairlie, and M. D. Wood. 2009. Parents do matter: A longitudinal two part mixed model of early college alcohol participation and intensity. *Journal of Studies on Alcohol and Drugs* 70:908–918.

Windle, M., L. P. Spear, A. J. Fuligni, A. Angold, J. D. Brown, D. Pine, G. R. Smith, J. Giedd, and R. E. Dahl. 2008. Transitions into underage and problem drinking: Developmental processes and mechanisms between 10 and 15 years of age. *Pediatrics* 121:S273–S289 (Supplement 4).

Chapter 4

Bandura, A. 1994. Social cognitive theory of mass communication. In *Media effects: Advances in theory and research*, eds. J. Bryant and D. Zillmann. Hillsdale, NJ: Lawrence Erlbaum Associates, 61–90.

Braun-Courville, D. K., and M. Rojas. 2009. Exposure to sexually explicit web sites and adolescent sexual attitudes and behaviors. *Journal of Adolescent Health* 45:156–62.

Gerbner, G., L. Gross, M. Morgan, and N. Signorielli. 1994. Growing up with television: The cultivation perspective. In *Media effects: Advances in theory and research*, eds. J. Bryant and D. Zillmann. Hillsdale, NJ: Lawrence Erlbaum Associates, 17–41.

Leinwand, D. 2007. Teens use internet to share drug stories. *USA Today*. http://www.usatoday.com/news/nation/2007-06-18-online_N.htm (accessed March 1, 2013).

Lo, V., and R. Wei. 2005. Exposure to Internet pornography and Taiwanese adolescents' sexual attitudes and behavior. *Journal of Broadcasting & Electronic Media* 49:221–37.

Mitchell, K. J., D. Finkelhor, and J. Wolak. 2003. The exposure of youth to unwanted sexual material on the Internet: A national survey of risk, impact, and prevention. *Youth & Society* 34:330–58.

Moreno, M. A., M. R. Parks, F. J. Zimmerman, T. E. Brito, and D. A. Christakis. 2009. Display of health risk behaviors on MySpace by adolescents: Prevalence and associations. *Archives of Pediatrics & Adolescent Medicine* 163:27–34.

Moreno, M. A., L. R. Briner, A. Williams, L. Walker, and D. A. Christakis. 2009. Real use or "real cool": Adolescents speak out about displayed alcohol references on social networking websites. *Journal of Adolescent Health* 45:420–21.

Rideout, V. J., U. G. Foehr, and D. F. Roberts. 2010. Generation M^2: Media in the lives of 8- to 18-year-olds. http://www.kff.org/entmedia/upload/8010 .pdf (accessed March 14, 2013).

Teen sets off bombs he learned to make on YouTube. September 13, 2010. KTLA News. http://www.ktla.com/news/landing/ktla-ione-bomb,0,1348 662.story (accessed August 1, 2012).

Wolak, J., K. Mitchell, and D. Finkelhor. 2006. Online victimization of youth: Five years later. http://www.unh.edu/ccrc/pdf/CV138.pdf (accessed March 14, 2013).

Wolak, J. D., K. J. Mitchell, and D. Finkelhor. 2007. Unwanted and wanted exposure to online pornography in a national sample of youth internet users. *Pediatrics* 119:247–57.

Ybarra, M. L., K. J. Mitchell, and J. D. Korchmaros. 2011. National trends in exposure to and experiences of violence on the Internet among children. *Pediatrics* 128:1376–86.

Chapter 5

Babchishin, K. M., R. K. Hanson, and C. A. Hermann. 2011. The characteristics of online sex offenders: A meta-analysis. *Journal of Sex Abuse* 23:92–123.

Centers for Disease Control and Prevention. 2011. 2011 youth risk behavior survey. http://www.cdc.gov/yrbs (accessed on August 4, 2012).

Menn, J. 2013. Reuters: Social networks scan for sexual predators, with uneven results. NBCnews.com. http://www.msnbc.msn.com/id/48161130/ns/tech nology_and_science-security/t/social-networks-scan-sexual-predators-un even-results/#.UBvcvfXhdIY (accessed March 14, 2013).

Miller, J. R. 2010. Chatroulette is "predator's paradise" experts say. Foxnews. com. http://www.foxnews.com/tech/2010/03/01/chatroulette-chock-legal -questions-attorneys-say/#ixzz22Q1lwgw9 (accessed March 14, 2013).

Mitchell K. J., D. Finkelhor, and J. Wolak. 2005. Protecting youth online: Family use of filtering and blocking software. *Child Abuse and Neglect* 29(7):753–65.

Moreno, M. A., L. N. Brockman, J. N. Wasserheit, and D. A. Christakis. 2012. A pilot evaluation of older adolescents' sexual reference displays on Facebook. *Journal of Sex Research* 49:290–99.

Selkie, E., M. Benson, and M. Moreno. 2011. Adolescents' views regarding uses of social networking websites and text messaging for adolescent sexual health education. *American Journal of Health Education* 42(4): 205–212.

Temple, J. R., J. A. Paul, P. van den Berg, V. D. Le, A. McElhany, and B. W. Temple. 2012. Teen sexting and its association with sexual behavior. *Archives of Pediatrics and Adolescent Medicine* 166:828–33.

Wolak, J., D. Finkelhor, and K. Mitchell. 2011. Child pornography possessors: Trends in offender and case characteristics. *Sex Abuse* 23(1): 22–42. doi: 10 .1177/1079063210372143.

Wolak, J., D. Finkelhor, and K. J. Mitchell. 2004. Internet-initiated sex crimes against minors: Implications for prevention based on findings from a national study. *Journal of Adolescent Health* 35(5): 424.e11–20.

Chapter 6

Craig, W. M., D. Pepler, and J. Blais. 2007. Responding to bullying: What works? *School Psychology International* 28:465–77.

Finn, J. 2004. A survey of online harassment at a university campus. *Journal of Interpersonal Violence* 19(3): 468–83.

Lenhart, A. 2007. Cyberbullying and online teens: Pew Internet and American Life Project. http://www.pewinternet.org/pdfs/PIP%20Cyberbullying%20 Memo.pdf (accessed June 2, 2012).

Li, Q. 2007. New bottle but old wine: A research of cyberbullying in schools. *Computers and Human Behavior* 23:1777–91.

Smith P. K., J. Mahdavi, M. Carvalho, S. Fisher, S. Russell, and N. Tippett. 2008. Cyberbullying: Its nature and impact in secondary school pupils. *Journal of Child Psychology and Psychiatry* 49(4): 376–85.

Chapter 7

Ashby, S. L., C. M. Arcari, and M. B. Edmonson. 2006. Television viewing and risk of sexual initiation by young adolescents. *Archives of Pediatrics and Adolescent Medicine* 160(4): 375–80.

Ashby, S. L., and M. Rich. 2005. Video killed the radio star: The effects of music videos on adolescent health. *Adolescent Medicine Clinics* 16(2): 371–93, ix.

Bandura, A. 1977. *Social Learning Theory*. New York: General Learning Press.

Bandura, A. 1986. *Social Foundations of Thought and Action: A Social Cognitive Theory*. Englewood Cliffs, NJ: Prentice Hall.

Brown, J. D. 2000. Adolescents' sexual media diets. *Journal of Adolescent Health* 27(2 Suppl): 35–40.

Childs, M. 2010. Facebook surpasses Google in weekly US hits for first time. *Businessweek*. http://www.businessweek.com/news/2010-03-17/facebook -surpasses-google-in-weekly-u-s-hits-for-first-time.html (accessed June 4, 2012).

Christofides, E., A. Muise, and S. Desmarais. 2009. Information disclosure and control on Facebook: Are they two sides of the same coin or two different processes? *Cyberpsychology, Social Networking and Behavior* 12(3): 341–45.

Collins, R. L., T. B. Kashdan, and G. Gollnisch. 2003. The feasibility of using cellular phones to collect ecological momentary assessment data: Application to alcohol consumption. *Experimental and Clinical Psychopharmacology* 11(1): 73–78.

Courtois, C., A. All, and H. Vanwynsberghe. 2012. Social network profiles as information sources for adolescents' offline relations. *Cyberpsychology, Behavior, and Social Networking* 15:290–95.

D'Angelo, J., and B. Van Der Heide. The formation of physician credibility ratings in online communities: Negativity, positivity, and non-normativity effects. *Communication Research* in Press, online version available at http://etd.ohiolink.edu/view.cgi?acc_num=osu1308324510.

Ellison, N. B., C. Steinfield, and C. Lampe. 2007. The benefits of Facebook "friends:" Social capital and college students' use of online social network sites. *Journal of Computer-Mediated Communication* 12:1143–68.

Escobar-Chaves, S. L., S. R. Tortolero, C. M. Markham, B. J. Low, P. Eitel, and P. Thickstun. 2005. Impact of the media on adolescent sexual attitudes and behaviors. *Pediatrics* 116(1): 303–26.

Fleming, P. J. 1990. *Software and sympathy: Therapeutic interaction with the computer.* Norwood, NJ: Ablex.

Fogg, B. J. 2008. *Mass interpersonal persuasion: An early view of a new phenomenon.* Third International Conference on Persuasive Technology. Berlin: Springer.

Gerbner, G., M. Gross, M. Morgan, and N. Signorelli. 1986. Living with television: The dynamics of the cultivation process. In *Perspectives on media effects,* eds. J. Bryant and D. Zillman. Hillsdale, NJ: Lawrence Erlbaum Associates: 17–40.

Gidwani, P. P., A. Sobol, W. DeJong, J. M. Perrin, S. L. Gortmaker. 2002. Television viewing and initiation of smoking among youth. *Pediatrics* 110(3): 505–508.

Google. 2010. Google Ad Planner. https://www.google.com/adplanner/planning/site_details#siteDetails?identifier=facebook.com&geo=US&trait_type=1&lp=false (accessed April 16, 2010).

Hinduja, S., and J. W. Patchin. 2008. Personal information of adolescents on the Internet: A quantitative content analysis of MySpace. *Journal of Adolescence* 31(1): 125–46.

Kluemper, D. H., and P. A. Rosen. 2009. Future employment selection methods: Evaluating social networking web sites. *Journal of Managerial Psychology* 24(6): 567–80.

Lenhart, A., K. Purcell, A. Smith, and K. Zickhur. 2010. Social media and young adults. Washington, DC: Pew Internet and American Life Project.

Litt, D. M., and M. L. Stock. 2011. Adolescent alcohol-related risk cognitions: The roles of social norms and social networking sites. *Psychology of Addictive Behaviors* 25:708–713.

Livingstone, S. 2008. Taking risky opportunities in youthful content creation: Teenagers' use of social networking sites for intimacy, privacy and self-expression. *New Media & Society* 10(3): 393–411.

Minteer, B. A., and J. P. Collins. 2008. From environmental to ecological ethics: Toward a practical ethics for ecologists and conservationists. *Science and Engineering Ethics* 14(4): 483–501.

Moreno, M. A., L. R. Briner, L. Williams, L. Walker, L. N. Brockman, and D. A. Christakis. 2009. Real use or "real cool": Adolescents speak out about displayed alcohol references on social networking websites. *Journal of Adolescent Health* 45(4): 420–22.

Moreno, M. A., L. N. Brockman, C. B. Rogers, and D. A. Christakis. 2010. An evaluation of the distribution of sexual references among "top 8" MySpace friends. *Journal of Adolescent Health* 47:418–20.

Moreno, M. A., M. Parks, and L. P. Richardson. 2007. What are adolescents showing the world about their health risk behaviors on MySpace? *Medscape General Medicine* 9(4): 9.

Moreno, M. A., M. R. Parks, F. Zimmerman, T. Brito, and D. A. Christakis. 2009. Display of health risk behaviors on MySpace by adolescents: Prevalence and associations. *Archives of Pediatrics and Adolescent Medicine* 163(1): 35–41.

Moreno, M. A., D. A. Christakis, K. G. Egan, L. N. Brockman, and T. Becker. 2012. Associations between displayed alcohol references on Facebook and problem drinking among college students. *Archives of Pediatrics and Adolescent Medicine* 166(2): 157–63. http://www.ncbi.nlm.nih.gov/pubmed/2196 9360 (accessed May 10, 2013).

Moreno, M. A., A. Grant, L. E. Kacvinsky, K. G. Egan, and M. F. Fleming. 2012. College students' alcohol displays on Facebook: Intervention considerations. *Journal of American College Health* 60(5):388–94.

Neinstein, L., and M. Anderson. 2002. Adolescent development. In *Adolescent Health Care: A Practical Guide,* ed. L. Neinstein. Philadelphia, PA: Lippincott Williams and Wilkins, 767–92.

Newman, M. G., A. Consoli, et al. 1997. Computers in assessment and cognitive behavioral treatment of clinical disorders: Anxiety as a case in point. *Behavioral Therapy* 28:211–35.

Pempek, T. A., Y. A. Yermolayeva, and S. L. Calvert. 2009. College students' social networking experiences on Facebook. *Journal of Applied Developmental Psychology* 30(3): 227–38.

Robinson, T. N., H. L. Chen, and J. D. Killin. 1998. Television and music video exposure and risk of adolescent alcohol use. *Pediatrics* 102(5): E54.

Sacerdote, B. 2001. Peer effects with random assignment: Results for Dartmouth College roomates. *The Quarterly Journal of Economics* 116(2): 681–704.

Strasburger, V. C., and B. J. Wilson. 2002. *Children, Adolescents and the Media.* Beverly Hills, CA: Sage Publications.

Subrahmanyam, K., S. M. Reich, N. Waechter, and G. Espinoza. 2008. Online and offline social networks: Use of social networking sites by emerging adults. *Journal of Applied Developmental Psychology* 29(6): 420–33.

Swatz, J. 2012. Facebook sees contenders in Pheed, CyPop, Myspace. *USA Today*, October 15, 2012.

Villiard, H., and M. A. Moreno. 2012. Fitness on Facebook: Advertisements generated in response to profile content. *Cyberpsychology, Behavior and Social Networking* 15(10): 564–68.

Wallace, P., S. Linke, E. Murray, J. McCambridge, and S Thompson. 2006. A randomized controlled trial of an interactive Web-based intervention for reducing alcohol consumption. *Journal of Telemedicine and Telecare* 12 Suppl 1:52–54.

Walther, J. B., and M. R. Parks. 2002. Cues filtered out, cues filtered in: Computer mediated communication and relationships. In *The Handbook of Interpersonal Communication*, eds. M. L. Knapp, J. A. Daly, and G. R. Miller. Thousand Oaks, CA: Sage Publications, 529–63.

Walther, J. B., B. Van Der Heide, L. Hamel, and H. Shulman. 2009. Self-generated versus other-generated statements and impressions in computer-mediated communication: A test of warranting theory using Facebook. *Communication Research* 36:229–53.

Chapter 8

Christakis, D. A., M. A. Moreno, L. A. Jelenchick, M. T. Myaing, and C. Zhou. 2011. Problematic Internet usage in US college students: A pilot study. *BMC Medicine* 9:77.

Christakis, D. A., and M. A. Moreno. 2009. Trapped in the net: Will Internet addiction become a 21st century epidemic? *Archives of Pediatric and Adolescent Medicine* 163(10): 959–60.

Jelenchick, L. A., T. Becker, and M. A. Moreno. 2012. Assessing the psychometric properties of the Internet Addiction Test (IAT) in US college students. *Psychiatry Research* 196(2–3): 296–301. http://www.ncbi.nlm.nih.gov/pubmed/22386568 (accessed May 10, 2013).

Moreno, M. A., L. A. Jelenchick, E. D. Cox, H. N. Young, and D. A. Christakis. 2011. Problematic Internet use among US youth: A systematic review. *Archives of Pediatrics and Adolescent Medicine* 165:797–805. PMC3215336.

Young, K. 1998. Internet addiction: The emergence of a new clinical disorder. *Cyberpsychology, Behavior and Social Networking* 1:237–44.

Chapter 9

Moreno, M. A., M. J. Swanson, H. Royer, and L. J. Roberts. 2011. Sexpectations: Male college students' views about displayed sexual references on females' social networking web sites. *Journal of Pediatric and Adolescent Gynecology* 25(2): 85–89.

Chapter 10

Deas, D., and E. S. Brown. 2006. Adolescent substance abuse and psychiatric comorbidities. *Journal of Clinical Psychiatry* 57(7): e02.

Egan, K. G., and M. A. Moreno. 2011. Prevalence of stress references on college freshman Facebook profiles. *Computer Information Nursing Journal* 29(10): 586–92.

Eisenberg, D., E. Golberstien, and S. E. Gollust. 2007. Help-seeking and access to mental health care in the university student population. *Medical Care* 45(7): 594–601.

Favaro, A., S. Ferrara, and P. Santonastaso. 2003. The spectrum of eating disorders in young women: A prevalence study in a general population sample. *Psychosomatic Medicine* 65(4): 701–708.

Garlow, S. J., J. Rosenberg, J. D. Moore, A. P. Haas, B. Koestner, H. Hendin, and C. B. Nemeroff. 2008. Depression, desperation, and suicidal ideation in college students: Results from the American Foundation for Suicide Prevention College Screening Project at Emory University. *Depression and Anxiety* 25(6): 482–88.

Hunt, J., and D. Eisenberg. 2010. Mental health problems and help-seeking behavior among college students. *Journal of Adolescent Health* 46(1): 3–10.

Jelenchick, L. A., J. C. Eickhoff, and M. A. Moreno. 2013. Facebook depression? Social networking site use and depression in older adolescents. *Journal of Adolescent Health* 52(1): 128–30.

Kessler, R. C., and C. L. Foster. 1995. Social consequences of psychiatric disorders I: Educational attainment. *The American Journal of Psychiatry* 152(7): 1026–32.

Mohnke, S., and P. Warschburger. 2011. Body dissatisfaction among female and male adolescents: Comparing prevalence, predictors and consequences between the sexes. *Praxis der Kinderpsychologie and Kinderpsychiatrie* 60(4): 285–303.

Moreno, M. A., D. A. Christakis, K. G. Egan, L. A. Jelenchick, E. D. Cox, H. N. Young, H. Villiard, and T. Becker. 2012. A pilot evaluation of associations between displayed depression references on Facebook and self-reported depression using a clinical scale. *Journal of Behavioral Health Services and Research* 39:295–304. PMC3266445.

Moreno, M. A., L. A. Jelenchick, K. G. Egan, E. D. Cox, H. N. Young, K. E. Gannon, and T. Becker. 2011. Feeling bad on Facebook: Depression disclosures on a social networking site. *Depression and Anxiety* 28:447–55. PMC3110617.

Pope, C., H. Pope, W. Menard, C. Fay, R. Olivardia, and K. Phillips. 2006. Clinical features of muscle dysmorphia among males with body dysmorphic disorder. *Body Image* 2(4): 395–400.

Quiles Marcos, Y., M. J. Quiles Sebastián, L. Panies Aubalat, J. Botella Ausina, and J. Treasure. 2013. Peer and family influence in eating disorders: A meta-analysis. *European Psychiatry* 28(4): 199–206.

Rao, U. 2006. Links between depression and substance abuse in adolescents: Neurobiological mechanisms. *Adolescent Journal of Preventative Medicine* 31(6): S161–S174.

Rao, U., and L. A. Chen. 2009. Characteristics, correlates, and outcomes of childhood and adolescent depressive disorders. *Dialogues of Clinical Neuroscience* 11(1): 45–62.

Rohde, P., N. Clarke, P. M. Lewinsohn, J. R. Seeley, and N. K. Kaufman. 2001. Impact of comorbidity on a cognitive-behavioral group treatment for adolescent depression. *Journal of American Academy of Child and Adolescent Psychiatry* 40(7): 795–802.

Stice, E., W. S. Agras, and L. D. Hammer. 1999. Risk factors for the emergence of childhood eating disturbances: A five year-prospective study. *International Journal of Eating Disorders* 25: 375–87.

Teagle, S. E. 2002. Parental problem recognition and child mental health service use. *Mental Health Services Research* 4(4): 257–66.

Vance, K., W. Howe, and R. P. Dellavalle. 2009. Social Internet sites as a source of public health information. *Dermatologic Clinics* 27(2): 133–35.

Yang, J. S., S. Yao, X. Zhu, C. Zhang, Y. Ling, J. R. Abela, P. G. Esseling, and C. McWhinnie. 2010. The impact of stress on depressive symptoms is moderated by social support in Chinese adolescents with subthreshold depression: A multi-wave longitudinal study. *Journal of Affective Disorders* 127(1–3): 113–21.

Chapter 11

Gentzler, A. L., A. M. Oberhauser, D. Westerman, and D. K. Nadorff. 2011. College students' use of electronic communication with parents: Links to loneliness, attachment, and relationship quality. *Cyberpsychology, Behavior and Social Networking* 14(1–2): 71–74.

Small, M. L., N. Morgan, C. Abar, and J. L. Maggs. 2011. Protective effects of parent–college student communication during the first semester of college. *Journal of American College Health* 59(6): 547–54.

« Resources »

How-To Resources for Parents

Facebook's Help Site
www.facebook.com/help
A great starting place to learn about is Facebook's help site, which provides information on starting an account, using Facebook, and privacy and security settings.

How Stuff Works—Facebook
http://computer.howstuffworks.com/Internet/tips/how-to-use-facebook.htm
This helpful website provides useful, detailed information on how to create a Facebook account, as well as on many of its features.

AARP's Guide to Social Networking
www.aarp.org/technology/how-to-guides/social-networking/?C-MP=KNC-360I-GOOGLE-TEC-HOW&HBX_PK=how_to_use_facebook
This interesting website provides tips on how to use many of Facebook's potentially confusing features.

General Internet Safety Resources for Parents

Pew Internet and American Life Project
http://pewinternet.org
A nonprofit "think tank" that conducts research and publishes reports. The Project focuses on the impact of the Internet on families and communities.

Common Sense Media
www.commonsensemedia.org
Common Sense Media is a nonprofit think tank dedicated to providing information and education related to media and technology.

SMAHRT website
www.smahrtresearch.com
Our research team's website includes details about our research studies, tips for

parents, information about our research team, and a section in which parents can submit questions.

In a research study conducted by our group, we evaluated a set of Internet safety websites using both quality and appeal criteria. Our goal was to identify the best quality websites out there, meaning the sites that had information that was accurate and easy to find. Websites that provided updated content, included the author's name and credentials, and provided references for their information had higher quality ratings than websites that didn't include these characteristics. We also wanted to identify websites that were appealing, including being easy to read and navigate, and relatively free of distractions and advertisements. The list of top websites includes:

www.safetyweb.com

www.onguardonline.gov

www.kidshealth.org

kids.getnetwise.org/safetyguide

safesurfingkids.com

wiredsafety.org

getsafeonline.org

Parents who are interested in learning more about how to identify inaccurate online information can begin by looking up the Center for Media Literacy or the National Association for Media Literacy Education. "Media literacy" describes the ability to search and find information online that is relevant and accurate. Some schools are now teaching this topic, and other websites provide models for teachers and parents to teach this important topic.

Center for Media Literacy: www.medialit.org

National Association for Media Literacy Education: http://namle.net

Sexual Health Resources for Parents and Teens

The following are websites we have reviewed and found to be comprehensive sources of information on topics of teen sexual health including pregnancy (and its prevention), sexually transmitted infection prevention and treatment, and relationships. These sites provide medically accurate information that is written for teens and young people in a relatable way. Most sites also have links to sites for parents that give tips on talking to your teen about sexual health. Browse through these sites yourself so you can help your teen decide how best to get their information.

Teen Wire

www.teenwire.org

A Planned Parenthood site for teens.

It's Your Sex Life

www.itsyoursexlife.com

An MTV-affiliated site with reputable information (your teen sees this link at the end of every episode of *16 and Pregnant* or *Teen Mom*).

Teens Health

www.teenshealth.org

A site run by Nemours, a children's health system with hospitals and clinics in multiple states.

Scarleteen

www.scarleteen.com

A site geared toward teens and young adults about sex and relationships, with contributions from educators, health care providers, clergy, and other disciplines.

Stay Teen

http://stayteen.org

A teen site from the National Campaign to Prevent Teen and Unplanned Pregnancy.

BUT! Stay Skeptical About

Yahoo! Answers

http://answers.yahoo.com

Millions of questions are asked, millions of questions are answered. By random users. Occasionally some of the answers to health related questions will be answered by a person that Yahoo! has verified is a doctor, nurse, or other health-care expert, but usually the answers are given by other Yahoo! users who may be just as clueless as your teen.

Wikipedia

http://en.wikipedia.org

Wikipedia is one of the trickiest sites for teens to navigate when looking for sexual health information. While much of the information in any Wikipedia article is accurate, keep in mind that ultimately this is a user-generated site and anyone can add to a page. Always check for citations in an article (and click through to make sure they're real sources).

Cyberbullying Resources

For Younger Teens
pacerteensagainstbullying.com
An interactive website that offers advice on how to prevent and deal with bullying, a section where celebrities talk about their experiences with bullying, and videos by and for teens.

stopcyberbullying.org
An informational website that has specific sections for tweens, teens, and older adolescents. It addresses both prevention and how to deal with bullies.

For Older Teens and College Students
athinline.org
Developed by MTV to raise awareness and provide resources about online harassment, this website offers teens helpful quizzes, advice, and perspectives from popular celebrities on cyberbullying and its harmful effects.

For Parents
wiredsafety.org
A good resource for parents who want to find out more about general online safety risks, and includes information and general advice.

stopbullying.gov
A very informative website that covers what cyberbullying is, who might be at risk, and how parents can help prevent and react to bullying. A lifeline phone number is given on the site, for situations that get out of hand.

Depression Resources for Parents

Youth Suicide Prevention Program Parent Guide
www.yspp.org/downloads/resources/YSPP_depression_Final_low.pdf

NASP (National Association of School Psychologists) pamphlet
www.nasponline.org/resources/handouts/revisedPDFs/depression.pdf

Helpguide
www.helpguide.org/mental/depression_teen.htm

Obesity Prevention Resources for Parents

The Center for Disease Control's website on obesity
www.cdc.gov/obesity
See the section on "For my family."

Let's Move

A website to promote physical activity for families as well as healthy recipes. www.letsmove.gov

Eating Disorder Resources for Parents

There are many prevention and intervention programs for eating disorders, including therapy, nutritional counseling, support groups, and residential treatment. NationalEatingDisorders.org offers toolkits for parents and offers a helpline at (800) 931-2237.

≪ Index ≫